The Complete Guide to
Writing A Successful
SCREENPLAY

*Everything You Need to Know
to Write and Sell a Winning Script*

Melissa Samaroo

THE COMPLETE GUIDE TO WRITING A SUCCESSFUL SCREENPLAY: EVERYTHING YOU NEED TO KNOW TO WRITE AND SELL A WINNING SCRIPT

Copyright © 2015 Atlantic Publishing Group, Inc.
1405 SW 6th Avenue • Ocala, Florida 34471 • Phone 800-814-1132 • Fax 352-622-1875
Website: www.atlantic-pub.com • E-mail: sales@atlantic-pub.com
SAN Number: 268-1250

Library of Congress Cataloging-in-Publication Data

Samaroo, Melissa, 1982-
   The complete guide to writing a successful screenplay : everything you need to know to write and sell a winning script / by Melissa Samaroo.
      p. cm.
   Includes bibliographical references and index.
   ISBN-13: 978-1-60138-607-6 (alk. paper)
   ISBN-10: 1-60138-607-9 (alk. paper)
   1. Motion picture authorship. 2. Motion picture plays--Marketing. I. Title.
   PN1996.S26 2012
   791.43'7--dc23
                           2012020949

Printed in the United States

Printed on Recycled Paper

A few years back we lost our beloved pet dog Bear, who was not only our best and dearest friend but also the "Vice President of Sunshine" here at Atlantic Publishing. He did not receive a salary but worked tirelessly 24 hours a day to please his parents.

Bear was a rescue dog who turned around and showered myself, my wife, Sherri, his grandparents Jean, Bob, and Nancy, and every person and animal he met (well, maybe not rabbits) with friendship and love. He made a lot of people smile every day.

We wanted you to know a portion of the profits of this book will be donated in Bear's memory to local animal shelters, parks, conservation organizations, and other individuals and nonprofit organizations in need of assistance.

– Douglas & Sherri Brown

PS: We have since adopted two more rescue dogs: first Scout, and the following year, Ginger. They were both mixed golden retrievers who needed a home.

Want to help animals and the world? Here are a dozen easy suggestions you and your family can implement today:

- *Adopt and rescue a pet from a local shelter.*
- *Support local and no-kill animal shelters.*
- *Plant a tree to honor someone you love.*
- *Be a developer — put up some birdhouses.*
- *Buy live, potted Christmas trees and replant them.*
- *Make sure you spend time with your animals each day.*
- *Save natural resources by recycling and buying recycled products.*
- *Drink tap water, or filter your own water at home.*
- *Whenever possible, limit your use of or do not use pesticides.*
- *If you eat seafood, make sustainable choices.*
- *Support your local farmers market.*
- *Get outside. Visit a park, volunteer, walk your dog, or ride your bike.*

Five years ago, Atlantic Publishing signed the Green Press Initiative. These guidelines promote environmentally friendly practices, such as using recycled stock and vegetable-based inks, avoiding waste, choosing energy-efficient resources, and promoting a no-pulping policy. We now use 100-percent recycled stock on all our books. The results: in one year, switching to post-consumer recycled stock saved 24 mature trees, 5,000 gallons of water, the equivalent of the total energy used for one home in a year, and the equivalent of the greenhouse gases from one car driven for a year.

Disclaimer

The material in this book is provided for informational purposes and as a general guide to writing a screenplay only. Basic definitions of laws are provided according to the status of the laws at the time of printing; be sure to check for a change or update in laws. This book should not substitute professional and legal counsel for selling your screenplay.

Author Dedication

For Gabriel, who is amazing,
and for my family, who helped to make him that way.

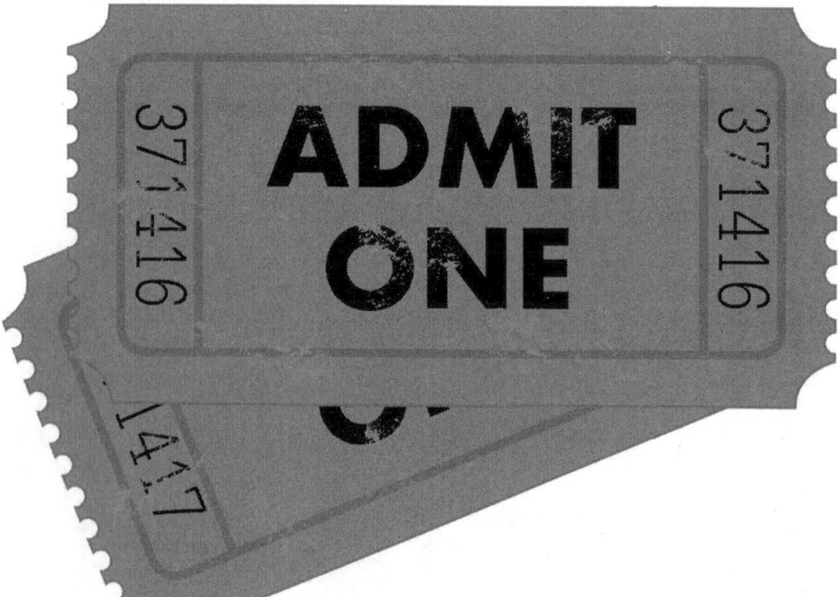
ADMIT
ONE
371416
371416

Table of Contents

Chapter 2: Learning From the Masters 35

Chapter 3: Developing a Story Concept 59

Chapter 4: Adapting an Existing Work 81

Chapter 8: Writing Up the First Draft, Scene by Scene 169

Chapter 9: Talking the Talk 191

Chapter 10: Emphasizing the Important Parts 205

Chapter 11: Developing Themes in Your Screenplay..........215

Chapter 12: Editing Your Screenplay....................................227

Chapter 13: Marketing Your Screenplay.....................................243

Chapter 14: Alternate Ways to Get A Movie Made..........................261

Introduction

These days, everyone wants to be a star. However, some people dream of more than appearing in front of the camera. Sure, the glitz and the glamour sound good. The paycheck must be nice. Compared to a regular nine-to-five job, the work seems easy. Reading a finished script and preparing to shoot a movie must be fun and glamorous. But wouldn't it be even better to craft the script?

For a writer, seeing his or her vision up on the big screen is the most rewarding experience, even if the movie is not a box office smash. Although the pay is certainly not that of a star, it is a sizeable amount. On average, a producer will pay between 2 and 5 percent of a movie's total budget for a screenplay, even one coming from a first-time screenwriter, according to the Writers Guild of America. With the average wide-released movie costing $65 million, according to the Motion Picture Association of America, you have the potential to bring in $3.25 million from one script.

Yet crafting a script, shaping the idea for a movie, is appealing for a different set of reasons. After the script is completed and sold, the director, producer, and actors all will have a say. The final product might vary from the plan set out in the original script. Still, the writer first determines each detail and aspect of the set and story.

Why the Writers' Strike?

When the WGA strike of 2007 to 2008 took hold, fans and viewers of popular television and movies got a good look at the writers who create these stories. Surprisingly, these people are not rich and famous. Most of them are ordinary writers who have succeeded at a dream many people hope to achieve.

The strike itself was over the writer's portion of the income earned by studios for the works they have written. Writers felt the studios were shortchanging them on their share from home video and Internet sales. The studios argued that they needed this money to make a profit and keep employing writers. The writers contended they needed the money to make it through periods of unemployment that are inherent in the contract nature of writing work: The studio will make the majority of the money. The writer will have to plan for times when there is no work.

What Does a Screenwriter Do?

The reality of being a screenwriter can be different from common perceptions about the job. Screenwriters write movies; this is true. But that is one of the many tasks they take on. Think about how many things writing accomplishes for the movie or TV show. It is more than the words the characters speak. It is creating full backgrounds and histories for the characters. In movies such as *The Family Stone* or *The Fighter*, when the characters happen to be one another's families, the screenwriter has to know the patterns of family interactions like a well-practiced dance. The screenwriter also must decide how many of that family's secrets should come out, when, and how.

Family movies often center around a special event or holiday, such as a wedding or Christmas. Though it might seem like over-kill, the screenwriter also should know all the details and plans around this special occasion before he or she sits down to write the movie. In a movie such as *The Matrix* or *Avatar* that takes place in an alternate universe, a screenwriter has to create a new world, along with its rules and laws, histories, and locations. The whole look of *Avatar*, from floating islands to blue people, was first laid out in the mind of James Cameron. Even a movie meant for teenagers, *Twilight* for example, can have elements of the su-pernatural that will need defining. The screenwriter has to decide not only the rules and laws that govern each supernatural crea-ture, but how to explain them to the audience.

On the opposite end of the spectrum, movies grounded in reality require extra time and effort through research. For movies featur-ing a particular career, the screenwriter might need to conduct research into the occupation. If the movie is set in a different peri-od, such as *The Secret Life of Bees* or *An Education*, the screenwriter will have to conduct research on the way people lived back then in order to write everything accurately from the lingo employed by people of the time to plausible actions taken by characters within the mindset of those eras. When viewers watch a movie, they notice details. If something in your screenplay is historically inaccurate and a viewer or reader knows it, it will take him or her out of the experience.

Making Mistakes in Public

Cataloguing errors in continuity as well as research, the Movie Mistakes website (**www.moviemistakes.com**) is a lazy filmmaker's nightmare. Viewers who pick up on the details ignored by filmmakers come together here. Users post screenshots that show items that are missing or different on a particular character's costume. They also discuss the errors caused by lack of research, such as military uniforms that do not display the proper signs of a character's rank.

In order to be successful, a screenwriter must be a master of many things. The script must be interesting enough to appeal to the reader from the first page. Not only does the writer have to write every word the actors will speak, but he or she also has to find the words to describe every detail that will appear on the screen. The appearance and styling of the characters have to be explained as well. But the screenwriter has to be mindful of the extent of his or her job and not step on the director's toes.

Most new screenwriters will end up submitting scripts to a slush pile of unsolicited manuscripts in an office, which likely will get read by readers or by the agent in their spare time. For a script to get noticed in a pile, it has to draw readers into the point where they can envision these elements in their minds.

Unlike writing a book or work of fiction, this is about more than creating descriptive sentences and precise words that weave a story together. It is also about creating visuals, setting up a picture that appeals to the eye. Some of the most famous and well-loved movie scenes would not be the same without the unique picture the words are spoken against.

Suppose one of your co-workers asked you to describe your home. Would you say "It's a white Victorian on First Street"? Or are you more likely to say "It's a white three-bedroom, two-bathroom Victorian-style house with green trim, two stories, a small front porch, a front yard with lots of grassy areas, and a long driveway"? You are not too likely to say the second one unless you are a real estate agent. You might mention whatever you feel is special and creates the most impact visually, such as if you have a large sitting porch or a big apple tree. But you are not going to bore your friend with a big long description. Similarly, you cannot bore a reader to death with an overlong description of the locations. Being a screenwriter is all about choosing the right words to make the most impact in the most succinct way.

How This Guide Can Help

Deciding to write a script is a commitment of a sizeable chunk of time. You will be anxious to finish your script, but it is hard to say how long it will take a first-time screenwriter. It can take months or even years to get your script to its best condition, the way it should be before you attempt to sell it. A creative endeavor, like a screenplay, often simply takes as long as it takes, and no amount of planning or guessing truly can tell you how long.

Because you will have to commit your time, which is the hardest commodity to find, you need to have a clear plan. At the outset, it might seem simple to write a movie. Maybe you have an idea that has been rattling around in your brain for a long time. How hard can it be to write it down? But composing a screenplay that is interesting and well paced all the way through is a complicated process. That kernel of an idea might have the potential to become a truly great screenplay, but it needs to be expanded, researched, and outlined before you can hope to create a whole screenplay out of it.

Knowing more about the business of screenwriting, what to expect, and how to prepare yourself for the industry can give you an edge over competitors who have not done the same research. This guide tries to give you a quick education on the whole process. Each aspect of writing a script is described. By reading this book before you begin your screenplay, or as you write it, you will be able to save yourself time and energy wasted by making errors.

Becoming a Screenwriter

Becoming a screenwriter is about more than the actual work of writing. To prepare yourself to work as a screenwriter, there is much to learn about the movie industry and the business end of screenwriting. Doing research and familiarizing yourself with how deals are made will help you know what to expect in the future. If you have never written anything before, do not panic. Good writers can be observant people from just about any walk of life.

Who Could Be a Good Screenwriter?

Because screenwriting is such a multifaceted business, any background can help. You might not think the experience you have can assist you in a new career as a screenwriter, but consider how the following backgrounds can help you craft a script:

- Parents have firsthand experience of the poignant moments in life to pull from when crafting scenes. Whether an awkwardly truthful comment from a toddler or a burst of anger from a teenager, parenting brings us into some emotionally charged moments.

- Writing a script that rings true to a viewer is all about making the dialogue and characters believable. People who deal with other people every day know how people talk and can draw on this experience to write convincing dialogue.

- Nurses and doctors get to see how people react at the most crucial times. When the pressure is on, the way people communicate with one another changes. When the situation becomes urgent, formalities and politeness go out the window. These moments can be the hardest to write without seeming trite or cliché.

- Business people have the savvy and know-how to network the right contacts and get their script to the right people. Networking and making the right contacts can be essential to selling your script much faster than soliciting through the slush pile.

No matter what background you come from, it helps to have some experience as a writer. It is not necessary to have written a screenplay before, but it helps to be able to craft sentences and to spell properly. If you hated writing in high school or college, do not worry too much. This is not an essay, and long compound sentences with fancy words are not needed. You do not need to impress anyone with your vocabulary. In a screenplay, short, direct sentences are best.

Qualities of a good screenwriter

No matter what background they come from, effective screenwriters share some qualities and traits:

- **Curiosity** — Often, the best ideas for a creative work come from the author wondering about something and deciding to write the answer. What would happen if a stay-at-home mom decided to sew her own superhero costume and fight crime between school pickups? What if a case of mistaken identity led to a foreign prince working as a rickshaw puller in New York City? Feeling the curiosity about this question and not letting that curiosity die, is what drives the screenwriter to continue to the end.

- **Research Skills** — In the age of Google™, when audiences can and will pull out their phones to check the accuracy of the smallest fact, it is harder than ever to get the viewer to suspend his or her disbelief and go with you on a fantastic journey. One way to combat losing your audience over a small inaccuracy is to do extensive research about the subject and location of your film. The ability to research via Internet, books, and fact-finding trips will help you at this stage.

- **Perceptiveness** — A good screenwriter must have an eye for detail. If you have a good memory, here is where those details will pay off. The more precise you can be in your script, the better the chance that other people will be able to visualize your movie in their imagination. The more you can show the audience instead of having to have a character tell them, the better. You want the audience to know a character is nervous? Study a nervous person, and incorporate his or her tics into your character.

- **Brevity** — Writers of other kinds of works can expand on their ideas. A novelist can write until the story is done. But screenwriters are forced to stick to a much shorter page count. This means screenwriters must learn how to communicate their message in a much shorter space. Extra words have no place on the page of a script.

- **Motivation** — It is no secret that writers can be first-class procrastinators. With only your dream and ambition to force you to work, you must have a strong work ethic and motivation to see the script through to completion. After the script is done, trying to sell the script also will be difficult to stay motivated through. Accept the feedback given to you, and use it to make your script stronger, even if it means undertaking another rewrite.

- **Dedication** — Screenwriting, like any other creative endeavor, can be a lonely pursuit. And though it might seem like a glamorous job, screenwriting involves hard work. The editing, rewriting, and final polish of a script can be tedious but are needed to bring your script up to professional quality and standard. If you hope to sell your script, there is still more work ahead as you research agents, prepare treatments and manuscripts, enter contests, and work on other marketing tools, such as short films and websites.

- **Adaptability** — Once your script is sold, you will have to work with collaborators to tailor the script. Many times, changes called notes will be recommended to you. A good screenwriter can accept these criticisms without being offended and incorporate the feedback to make the overall script stronger. Being diplomatic about which changes can be made and which are unacceptable to you can make a difference in getting hired again.

- **Vision** — A good screenwriter needs to be able to craft an image and a character. For some, this can mean crafting backgrounds and biographies for their characters. Others take the time to sketch out the floor plan of their characters' homes and main locations of the script. For the writer to write convincingly about a story or a locale, it is important to be able to see all aspects of the situation.

You might have honed some of these skills in school or in your existing career. Some of these are natural traits that might not be in your personality. Do not panic if you do not possess all of these qualities right now. As you spend more time writing and editing your script, you will find yourself learning and growing more comfortable. You will find you possess many other qualities that can assist you in your screenwriting, and you will be able to build up any skills you are lacking.

Getting in the Habit of Writing

Writing can be a hard habit to get into. Even those who have a talent and passion for writing often find it hard to put in the daily work. It is easier to claim you are writing a screenplay than to write one. Some writers find they spend too much time talking to friends and acquaintances about their new endeavor. Others keep coming up with new ideas, each better than the last. Getting distracted from one idea by a so-called better one can be a way to keep you from finishing anything.

One of the biggest setbacks for new writers is staying dedicated to something that does not produce the same results each day. If you get on the treadmill for half an hour, you will burn a set amount of calories. But you can write for half an hour one day and get 200 words, feel really inspired the next day and get 500, and have writer's block the day after that and only squeak out 50. This frustrating difference in results can discourage you and make you want to quit. However, as you practice writing each day, you will see your results level out and become more consistent. Set yourself a goal of how many words you want to write that day, and increase it slowly as you go along.

Find inspiration everywhere

Remaining engaged with your screenplay during the day is another way to encourage the craft to take up residence in your life. Think about your screenplay even when you are not writing.

Allow visually exciting things you see throughout the day to find a place in your work. Maybe a flash mob appears in your subway station. The same can happen in your movie, as long as it advances the plot.

Keep a notebook with you — you never know when these inspirations will strike. Even if you only jot down one or two sentences, these can help you fight writer's block. When you do sit down for writing time, having a start on paper will help you get inspired right away. As you become more involved in the writing of your script, you might find that your characters speak to you. Jotting down a piece of dialog you hear from them now can inspire a whole paragraph when you sit down with it later.

Holding on to your Ideas

Many writers feel the ideas that come to them in strange places are the best ones. It is the same principle as those times you search for the name of a particular actor, then shortly after, you are driving down the road, and it comes to you. Your mind will keep working on the problems with your script long after you put it down, and the solution to something might come to you as you push your cart down the aisle at the grocery store. If you do not have a notebook when inspiration strikes, what can you do?

Because we live in a wired world, it is easy to keep track of your ideas. Iff it is short, send yourself a text or email.

Most smart phones have a note pad application that can be downloaded. This is an ideal place to jot down your ideas for future reference. You can also leave yourself a voice mail, but be prepared to sit patiently and listen to the playback while you type the message out.

The lonely life of a writer

Writing can be a lonely pursuit, which drives some people away. Forcing yourself to sit down each day in a quiet area does not sound like much fun. It can be difficult and frustrating to work through the issues associated with writing a full script without having someone to consult when you get stuck. If you are the type of person who prefers to work with someone, try building a network of writer friends or enlisting a writing buddy.

You do not need to go to film school to be a screenwriter. However, if you feel inclined to take a class or two in screenwriting, it could not hurt, and you might find a support group to help advise you on the problems in your second act or a severe case of writer's block.

Local community colleges or universities often offer this kind of class through their community education programs. If that is not an option, you can audit a college-level class. You can discuss your observations with the other students and hear what they took away from the same film. In a classroom setting, you might meet other people with an interest in screenwriting, potential writing buddies, or even just friends.

You also can find the support of other screenwriters online. Writing groups, forums, and critique circles are all places writers meet online to discuss and help each other with scripts in progress. Blogs and other resource websites exist where working screenwriters offer wisdom and advice. A writing group is usually just what it says: a group of writers that provide support to each other by meeting regularly. Forums are where you can post a question, get different answers from participants, and then decide which is the best one. Websites like **www.meetup.com** also can help you meet other people who are interested in working on the same type of work. Usually, a monthly meetup is held in a local area, at a coffee shop or park, for you to meet and discuss with other people who have indicated an interest. *Chapter 13 will have more on finding a writing buddy and ways to combat loneliness and beat writer's block.*

Staying committed to screenwriting

Like any new pursuit, at first you will be eager to spend time working on your script. It will seem fun and exciting, something you wish you had tried much sooner. But as time passes, the words stop flowing as easily and your personal life starts to demand more of your time. Chances are you will find yourself less excited about slogging through your pages. This is where it is important to stick with it. Screenwriting, if it is going to be your new career, has to be taken seriously.

Writing is a form of self-employment, and your only boss is you. If you hope to follow through, you have to take it as seriously as you would any other job. Instead of a hobby, it has to become a habit. Incorporate screenwriting into your day: Make it a routine to sit down and write every day at the same time. If you have a family or roommates, make it known that you would rather not be disturbed during this time. If you are easily distracted, programs available for download can block the use of your Internet browser during the time you are working on your writing. Find what makes you most comfortable and allows you the best work. Most people who set out to write a screenplay never end up finishing, so set that as your first goal. Seeing the goal through to completion can be your motivation to keep going and get your script sold.

Yoga for your Writer Muscles

Writing is mental exercise. It takes effort and concentration, and it can be draining. Like working out, strive to write a little every day, around the same time. Minimize the distractions in your writing area, or try listening to some music through headphones if you cannot find a quiet space. Optimize working conditions in your environment by experimenting with better lighting. To keep your brain ready and sharp, do a little writing each day. As you continue to practice, you will see your daily word count increase. Keep track of your word count and increase it a little each week or month. The more seriously you take this time, the more productive you will become.

How to Adapt Your Writing Style

If you are used to writing fiction or nonfiction, a screenplay will be different. You will encounter problems you never had writing in another medium. If you have experience as a writer, you already know the satisfaction of completing a project. Use this memory to push you forward as you work on the screenplay.

Fiction writers

Going from writing fiction to writing a screenplay is an exercise in control. While fiction writers are used to using as many words as needed to get a job done, a screenwriter has to accomplish the same thing in a much smaller number of pages. The method used to outline a screenplay is also different from the conventional method

used to outline a fiction work. Many fiction writers work without an outline or with a minimal outline. However, working on a screenplay without first outlining it is a recipe for disaster. There is so much to keep track of in a screenplay that starting one without properly outlining it first rarely works out well.

Nonfiction writers

A nonfiction writer also has to exercise control. Normally, a nonfiction work is a showcase for all the research the writer has done. In a screenplay, that research has to be woven into the script in different ways. Rather than listing the information for the reader to review, you have to incorporate the interesting facts into your scripts.

For example, you have decided to set your movie in Boston. After doing some research, you decide the characters live in Back Bay because the neighborhood is architecturally significant, popular with young professionals, and peppered with expensive shops. How can you convey this information to the viewer? In a non-fiction work, you simply could explain how the neighborhood came to its current demographic. In a script, you will have to come up with creative ways to show your audience all you want them to know. Maybe your characters live in one of Back Bay's signature brownstones. Or maybe they have an interest in the arts and visit the museums around the neighborhood during the course of the movie. As they walk down the street, the audience will take in the fancy shops and architectural landmarks you place in the background. Unlike with a nonfiction work, in which you try to give the reader every tidbit you can, screenwriting is about choosing the right tidbits, the ones that will tell the viewers the most. The locations you choose are the canvas in the background of your picture, while the details you provide will fill in everything in between.

The Business Side

Because writing is a creative pursuit, or maybe something you use as a creative outlet, it can be easy to forget it is a business. If you always have worked a conventional nine-to-five job, you will have to readjust your expectations for work in this field. Breaking into screenwriting requires you to have a lot of belief in yourself, as the process of selling your first script will be strange and somewhat disheartening.

The way scripts are sold

If you have never sold a script, familiarize yourself with the steps of the business before deciding if you want to undertake this task. Screenwriting is a lot of up-front work. You have to do this work on the faith that you will succeed, as you will not see any payment for it until long after it is complete.

There are different avenues to selling a script. Most first-time screenwriters solicit agents by submitting their manuscripts. However, Hollywood agents receive so many unsolicited manuscripts that they cannot read them all. They have readers whose jobs are to read scripts, hoping to find a hit. One of your jobs as a screenwriter is to grab the attention of one of those readers. Tired, bored, and ready to toss your script aside as soon as they give it the obligatory glance, readers have no reason to prefer your script to any other unless it is better than all of them. Though this is the most popular way to get a script sold, this is difficult, and an unknown screenwriter should expect many rejections before getting an acceptance.

Another avenue to selling your script is to enter it in screenwriting contests. Many of these contests exist, sometimes in connection with a larger event, such as a film festival. The contests that use agents, producers, and influential insiders as judges can help you with the difficult task of getting your script into the hands of someone who works in Hollywood.

Writers who have a friend or contact to help have a distinct advantage. If you do not know anyone who could help you, now is the time to begin networking and reaching out to friends and relatives. You might be surprised which of your friends knows someone who can help you out.

Should you actually sell your script, you can expect to be paid. If the film is released, and successful, you might see residual income in the future. *More on the business and how to sell your scripts is available in Chapter 11 of this guide.*

Learning From the Masters

*M*ost people have never seen a Hollywood script because they have never had the chance or the inclination. If this is the product you hope to create, examine it carefully. Some scripts are highly guarded, either by the writer who fears criticism or theft, or by the studio that owns the rights. Christopher Nolan, writer of the movie *Inception*, kept the details of his script secret during the filming to enhance the surprise for moviegoers. Mel Gibson did the same with the script of *Apocalypto*. But most scripts are easily available now via the Internet.

Websites exist with many scripts listed from different periods. There are many different editions of each script, and you might see these different types of scripts listed on each website. When you choose one to read, try to review submission stage scripts, as that is what you will be producing. Later editions of scripts, like shooting scripts, have more camera directions, which you do not need to include at this point.

Looking over the scripts of Hollywood movies and researching the market for your movie can help you get a better picture of the road ahead. It also can help you set realistic expectations for how long it will take to break into the business and how much money you can expect to make.

Read the scripts of successful movies, your favorite movies, even a few movies you really hated. Try to take in scripts from every genre and many different writers, from unknowns to celebrated household names. The more you can get used to the look of a page of script, the better.

Reading Screenwriting Online

Many resources are available online for potential screenwriters to learn about the industry. Screenwriters, readers, agents, and other Hollywood insiders all keep blogs revealing the inner workings of studios. You can learn about the everyday life of screenwriters, the business of Hollywood, and how to improve your script. Use this as a way to manage your expectations of your future career. Screenwriting is not glamorous, especially not at first. It is hard work and can be high pressure, with deadlines to meet. At the same time, remember to check who keeps these websites and blogs. Someone who has already made it in the industry has a much easier time finding work than you will. A first-time screenwriter might be relatable at this stage of your career but would not have any experience to offer.

Whether to keep up with what is currently happening in Hollywood is a question up for debate. Some people think keeping up with what is purchased in Hollywood and for how much only will hamper you. As you try to write your screenplay, what is selling right now should be the farthest thing from your mind because the trends will change before you finish the script. Others say it is good to know who the power players are and where they are spending money. Perhaps the best solution here is balance, to follow the trades but not religiously and only for general information, not to analyze and change your screenplay.

When you are ready to research scripts, you also can do this online. Many websites are available that offer copies of well-known movie scripts for aspiring screenwriters to read and review. Podcasts and news radio shows offer interviews with screenwriters about current works and classics. For example, sites such as SimplyScripts (**www.simplyscripts.com**), Drew's Script-O-Rama (**www.script-o-rama.com**) and the Internet Movie Script Database (**www.imsdb.com**) all have many popular movies in script form that you can read. Also, the website Trigger Street Labs (**http://labs.triggerstreet.com**) is a great community to join if you want to read scripts from beginning screenwriters just like you.

The sheer amount of free information available is a wonderful thing. But it also can be detrimental. Try to review a little of everything you feel will be useful to you, but avoid spending too much time getting lost in the depth of information. Researching too much is a particularly clever form of procrastination because something of merit still is done, but you need to limit your research to a certain amount of time. Consider ways to keep up with the sites you like without having to take the time to visit the actual site and look up the information you seek. See if the site offers an application for your mobile device, if you can subscribe to the site via RSS feed, or if you can follow the site on Twitter® or like them on Facebook®. Many sites still offer a mailing list you can get on to get regular email updating you. This way, the newest information and posts to the site will come directly to you.

The easy availability of this wealth of information also makes the people reading your script less tolerant of mistakes in your submission. If you cannot be bothered to get online and research, they will reason that you are not truly committed to the amount of work necessary. Thus, research into the submission guidelines of each place you submit to is critical. Making sure you eliminate the obvious errors from your submissions will keep you from getting eliminated in the early stages.

Screenwriting Bibles

Some books have been such institutions in the business of screenwriting that they have been popular for 20-plus years and are considered required reading for new screenwriters. Robert McKee's *Story: Substance, Structure, Style and the Principles of Screenwriting* was written back in the 1980s. The book examines how all the elements of a script work together to create a story. McKee created the accompanying story seminar, a live presentation of his principles, at around the same time. The seminar is now a four-day event in locations as far flung as Beijing, Moscow, and Hyderabad, with a cost of around $800. Some criticize McKee's credentials to teach, as he is not himself a well-known screenwriter; he has had a few sales but no big Hollywood credits. However, many well-known screenwriters, such as Peter Jackson, have found value in his teachings. Michael Hauge has enjoyed similar success with his book *Writing Screenplays That Sell*. Hauge takes a different approach to the structure of screenplays by explaining when events need to happen in percentages.

New screenwriters should read scripts for a few reasons. First, the process will help you to understand the format and exactly what needs to be on the page. Though the format of a script is similar to that of a stage play, stage directions should be omitted, as the director and actors will collaborate on the movement and blocking of a scene. Dictating camera shots is also something a screenwriter should avoid. You get few words in a script. Why waste any on what you know will likely be ignored?

Next, pay attention to the way the script is written. In screenwriting, there should be a lot of white space on the page. If you are used to writing fiction or nonfiction, it might take some time for you to adjust to the look of a page of script. See the sample below:

INT-OFFICE-DAY

Sara and Mary stand at the copier. Sara looks around to see if anyone is nearby while Mary jabs randomly at the buttons.

> MARY
> Do you think they know?

> SARA
> Who?

> MARY
> All of them!

> SARA
> How would they know?

> MARY
> James saw us. On the security camera. It's only
> a matter of time before they all know.

The copier begins to make a buzzing noise. Both girls take a step back but otherwise ignore it.

> SARA
> Why are you just now telling me this?

The copier beeps and starts spitting out paper.

> MARY
> I just found out. I couldn't very well come run-
> ning right to your desk.

Keeping the page clean

As seen in the sample page above, few words appear on each page of script. A good screenwriter must strike the right balance between the amount of dialogue on the page and the description. Because so few words appear on the page of a script, making each word count is important. The average Hollywood script is about 100 pages long. Each page of script represents one minute on screen. As a new writer, having a script that runs any longer than that is going to work against you when you try to sell it. More established writers can push this limit a bit, but the first thing any reader reviewing a new screenwriter's submission will think is that it is too long. If the movie you hope to write is for children or a family audience, try to get it down even further to 90 pages. Everything in the story needs to resolve itself well enough for the audience to feel satisfied without rushing, but if you can keep your script lean and trim, it will make a good impression.

Reading scripts also will help you get an idea of the pacing of a script. *More specific details on the structure of a script are found later in Chapter 3.* But at this stage, before you tackle the structure of your script, study where the action begins and ends in some famous scripts. Examine the structure of each scene, particularly the ones you find funny or touching. What is it about the scene that works so well? Is it the way the characters speak to each other? Is it the way long-running setups are paid off? Try to isolate what about the script makes the scene necessary. Soon, you will examine the scenes in your own script in this fashion to determine which should go. Keep in mind as you read that each character in the scene has his or her own distinct ambition, something he or she wants to get out of the conversation. How do you determine what that motivation is? What spoken clues and physical cues does the writer give?

Script reading checklist

As you read each script, here is a list of questions to ask yourself:

√   Who is the main character?

√   What does he or she want to achieve?

√   What will he or she do to get it?

√   Who is trying to prevent the main character from getting what he or she wants?

√   Why does this person want to stop the hero?

√   What nonverbal clues does the writer give to this person's personality?

√   Is the love story in this movie convincing? Why or why not?

√   What do you find charming about the love interest character?

√   What clues does a screenwriter give you about the bad traits of the love interest?

√   Do all of the setups in the script pay off?

√   Does the end resolve all the plotlines?

√   Is there any ambiguity in the ending? Do you think this was done intentionally?

Writing for Television

At the outset, writing for television might seem more appealing to a writer. Unfortunately, breaking into television can be even harder than Hollywood. Before creating a television show based on the concept all his or her own, a writer can expect to put in years of work. Most television shows are created and written by writers who already have established themselves in cinema or television.

Watching and Analyzing Movies

You can take the watching of movies seriously by printing out the script and taking notes of each important moment. However, watching movies is fun, and if you take all the fun out of it at this early stage, you will find it difficult to stay motivated throughout the process. The first time you watch the movie, it is better to watch it undistracted all the way through. Then, if there are parts you enjoyed or scenes you thought were done effectively, go back and look up the script online.

An Introduction to Film class can teach you basic concepts that will help you better understand how your script will translate to the screen. Understanding what a director of photography or a Foley artist does will help you to envision all the pieces that have to come together to produce a movie. Many film classes will screen classic movies. This will help you learn the process of analyzing a movie, breaking down the theme and story line, and what creates a visual impact to a viewer.

Continuing to watch movies is an important part of research. If you have read the script of a movie, you can compare the script to the finished product, but bear in mind the script might have had many revisions, as well as cuts from the director and changes or lines improved by the actors. A shooting script will be the final version of the script, but it can be confusing to a new writer to read this type of script, as it contains many things the writer does not need to include in a submission script.

You also can draw on the knowledge you have amassed through-out your lifetime. No doubt, you have seen movies of each genre. By now, you must have some idea of what kind of movies you prefer and which you do not care for. Now is the time to think about why that is. *Picking a genre for your screenplay will be discussed in Chapter 3.*

Writing on the Screen

Many movies over the years have centered on screenwriters. Here are two that were celebrated for their stories:

- *Barton Fink* (1991) — The Coen brothers, a critically acclaimed American duo, wrote this drama about a 1940s playwright who struggles to write movie scripts.

- *Adaptation* (2002) — Screenwriter Charlie Kaufman tells his story of the difficulty of adapting an existing work. Nicolas Cage and Meryl Streep starred in the movie.

Analyzing the movies you like

Everyone has at least a handful of movies he or she likes better than any others. Take a closer look at certain parts of these movies to see what they have in common:

- The look: Some movies just suit our mood, such as holiday movies with images of swirling snow, presents piled high, and kids waiting for Santa. Plenty of families live in snowless climates, but few holiday movies take place there. In *Home Alone*, the action takes place in their suburban neighborhood, decorated for Christmas. *Twilight*, the teenage romance phenomenon, takes place in Forks, Washington, the real-life rainiest place in America. The constant rainfall combined with the blue overtones of the light give the movie its creepy atmosphere. *Mamma Mia* showcases the upbeat songs of ABBA against a beautiful Grecian island. The singing and dancing against the beautiful blue of the ocean makes the audience feel as though they have gone on a carefree vacation with girlfriends.

- The communication style: Some people prefer a fast-talking, slick movie in which the dialogue flies so fast you still notice new things on the third or fourth viewing. Others like a slower pace, where each character takes time to evolve and speak his or her heart, such as what takes place in a Nicholas Sparks romance.

- The opening: Some movies throw the viewer directly into the action. *Pulp Fiction* starts with a couple talking in a diner, but within minutes, they are robbing it. This establishes the frantic pace that builds through the rest of the movie. Other films begin by showing the audience a day in the life of the characters. At the beginning of *Thelma and Louise*, the girls are going about their usual business. Thelma is trying to avoid confrontation with her controlling husband, while Louise waits tables at her dead-end job. The writer has shown us a day in their lives so we can see how much it will change.

- The style of humor: Movies such as *American Pie* or *Knocked Up* use a raunchier style of humor that shows or talks about taboo subjects or disgusting situations. Romantic comedies often have a clumsy but cute heroine who provides the film with humor by embarrassing herself. Renee Zellweger in the *Bridget Jones's Diary* franchise fell into a lake, landed rear end first onto a television camera, and said embarrassing things whenever she was in front of a group of people.

What's wrong with the movies you hate?

Few things irritate an audience more than a movie that does not deliver. In today's economy, wasting the price of a ticket on a lackluster movie hurts worse than ever. Some common problems that make movies bad:

The Same Old Story

Some complain that action movies are all the same. Maybe you dislike romantic comedies because you feel they are too predictable. Although a movie does require a certain structure, you can avoid this type of predictability by coming up with new and innovative takes on a scene. Remember, your characters have to accomplish things in each scene, but it does not have to be in the same way we have seen so many times before. One example of a romantic comedy that tries to accomplish this in premise is *What Happens In Vegas*. In this version, the boy and girl meet and drunkenly marry, and then one wins a Vegas jackpot of $1 million. Desperate to each hold on to his or her share, they try to run each other out of their shared house.

The Phony Talk

One of the reasons writing good dialogue presents such a challenge is because it is difficult to do. Often, you only notice bad dialogue. It takes you out of the moment because it is jarring to your ear. Whether a piece of dialogue works can vary based on the audience. Teenagers find a different kind of language relatable than adults. One example of a film known for its bad dialogue is *Showgirls*, winner of the Golden Raspberry Award for Worst Screenplay of the Year 1995. The film follows Nomi Malone, an aspiring Las Vegas dancer, on a sex-and-drama-filled rise to the top. Nomi hopes to become like Cristal Connors, the headlining dancer at the Stardust Hotel, whom she meets by chance. They have the following conversation:

> CRISTAL:
> I've had dog food.

> NOMI:
> You have?

> CRISTAL:
> Mmm-hmmm. Long time ago. Doggy Chow.
> I used to love Doggy Chow.

> NOMI:
> I used to love Doggy Chow, too!

Bad dialogue can be a problem for even the most acclaimed filmmaker. George Lucas, creator of *Star Wars*, has been called incapable of writing convincing dialogue. In *Episode II: Attack of The Clones*, Padme and Anakin talk about old times.

> PADME:
> We used to come here for school retreat. We would
> swim to that island every day. I love the water. We
> used to lie out on the sand and let the sun dry us
> and try to guess the names of the birds singing.

> ANAKIN:
> I don't like sand. It's coarse and rough and irritat-
> ing, and it gets everywhere. Not like here. Here
> everything is soft and smooth.

Many common mistakes render dialogue unconvincing, and you can try exercises to make your dialogue better as you learn more. *Some tips for writing dialogue will be covered in Chapter 9.*

Talking Heads

Every good scene in a movie should accomplish one primary function: to propel the main character along on his or her journey. More often than not, a scene will center around two or more of your characters talking. Keep your story visually interesting by changing the setting of the conversation:

- *When Harry Met Sally* — Sally tells Harry she would rather not strike up more of a friendship as they walk and stop on the moving sidewalk in the airport. It keeps the conversation visually interesting.

- *The 40-Year-Old Virgin* — Andy and his co-workers sit in the back alley of their workplace and hit each other in the pants with fluorescent light bulbs. Why? No explanation is given besides a level of understandable workplace boredom.

- *Sex and The City* — Over the years, the girls did a lot of gabbing all around New York City. Often, they sat in a coffee shop or restaurant as they worked their way through the day's dilemma. But these scenes were balanced with scenes of the girls all over town.

Controversial Ambiguous Endings

Perhaps you do not hate one particular genre but one particular type of ending. Ambiguous endings, in which viewers are not told what happened and have to interpret or create their own endings, work for some people. But many viewers prefer an ending in which all the story lines are resolved. This does not mean a happy ending for every character, just that his or her story comes to a clear ending.

Ambiguous endings, when the character's future is left to the viewer to decide, are controversial. Popular TV series *The Sopranos* generated a lot of opposition for the series finale, which ended with a simple cut to black that left viewers with the insinuation that main character Tony Soprano's life was about to end. Fans and media erupted over the lack of a clear ending, which series creator David Chase later said he had in mind for years. Just a touch of ambiguity, though, seems to work for audiences: The end of celebrated classic *Pulp Fiction* left the mystery of the briefcase's content. Fans still engage in debate online about exactly what the characters were protecting throughout the movie's events.

Deus Ex Machina

Viewers do not like a forced happy ending either. They have to feel the ending has been set up properly and has not been rushed to a conclusion.

Although the Greeks passed down many wonderful artistic traditions to us, they also passed down the deus ex machina, an ending in which a solution that pleases all drops out of the sky and magically ends the story. The term itself translates to "god out of the machine." In the Greek times, just as the story began to heat up and it seemed there was no way out, a god would appear on stage and set everything right. The best way for you to combat this is to introduce characters and plot points early on.

Tropes and the continued search for an original story

Over the years, it has all been written and said before. We all know the clichés and conventions that make a movie predictable. The wiki website tvtropes (**http://tvtropes.org**) exists for fans to catalog the appearance of tropes in television and other media.

A trope is something that viewers have seen before. Though there is some debate as to exactly what the term means, on this site the word trope refers to a writing device that has been overused to the point that viewers can recognize it. These tricks of the trade are useful for advancing the plot, which is why they have been used so much.

Sometimes fans laugh at screenwriters, and sometimes they laugh at themselves. As viewers have gotten savvier about tropes, some television shows such as *The Simpsons* have skewed them for laughs. *The Simpsons* has a Halloween episode each year, called the "Treehouse of Horror," an anthology of short scary stories.

Movies have often taken a crack or two at tropes of a certain genre, such as *Army of Darkness*, which skews the sci-fi and fantasy genres, and *The Princess Bride*, which takes sly swipes at fairy tales. In the 2000s, a whole line of movies was born out of making fun of standard movie plot devices: *Scary Movie, Not Another Teen Movie, Dance Movie,* and *Epic Movie*. These movies stack one trope after another, horrifying critics but grossing millions at the box office as audiences found them silly and enjoyable. For example, *Scary Movie* makes fun of the horror genre, which is loaded with tropes. The girls in the movie run up the stairs to get away from villains, the virgin dies last, and, perhaps the most well-known horror trope, the villain refuses to die, surviving to come back and lunge at the hero one or two or many more times. And who has not seen a movie or two or ten in which the villain offers a long, drawn-out speech during which the hero manages to escape?

Writers also joke with the audience through Easter eggs and winks. An Easter egg can be an inside joke or a hidden message of some kind inside the movie. One of the best-known Easter eggs is the Hidden Mickey. Hidden Mickey Mouse profiles, ranging from the three circle ears and head, to the classic profile of

Mickey's ears and nose in silhouette, to a full body Mickey, can be found hidden throughout Disney movies. Though they have never stated this as the purpose, finding Hidden Mickeys can keep grown-ups entertained through the tenth or 11th viewing of the children's favorite movie. Some examples of where you can find Hidden Mickeys:

- In the background of the street Lightning McQueen has to repave before he can leave radiator springs in *Cars*. One of the shops has signs outside that make up the three-circle Mickey head.

- Behind the Pevensie siblings on the wall in Mr. Tumnus' house in *The Chronicles of Narnia: The Lion, The Witch and the Wardrobe*

- In the sky as Mufasa gives Simba the speech on what it means to be a king during *The Lion King*

- In the trees as Mr. Incredible lands on the island in *The Incredibles*

The Cheater's Guide to the History of Film

So many classic films, so little time. Trying to watch the best films can be time consuming, and even if you had nothing but time, it would take you years. Still, you do not want to be totally in the dark about cinematic classics and masters. Familiarizing yourself with classic cinema will help you understand where the precedents of cinema come from, what has been done, and what is your real taste. The following is a simple overview from the Golden Age of Hollywood to the current climate of cinema around the world.

A brief history of Hollywood

The 1930s to the 1960s was the Golden Age of Hollywood. During this time, the movie studios took larger and more pronounced roles than they do today. Specific movie stars often were contracted to be in the films of only one studio. Movies of different genres were made, but each movie adhered strictly to the formula of that genre. All movies willingly adhered to the **Hays Code**, a form of moral code first enforced in 1934, rather than face legal action.

The Hollywood industry decided to protect itself from government censorship by censoring itself. The Hays Code dictated the behaviors that were acceptable to show on film. Among the conventions of this code was a necessary on-screen punishment for any criminals or anyone seen doing anything immoral. Revenge, drugs, alcohol, and murder were all out of the question unless punished, and even then, they could be banned. Homosexuality could not be discussed, nor could religious questions.

Anyone who tells you that Ilsa was supposed to stay in *Casablanca* with Rick is a film novice. Due to the Hays Code, Ilsa could not have left her husband for another man.

The Best American Film of All Time?

Critics and moviegoers alike have named Orson Welles' epic *Citizen Kane* as the best film of all time. Orson Welles co-wrote and starred as Charles Foster Kane, a reclusive millionaire searching for his lost childhood. The structure of the film defied Hollywood conventions at the time, as it jumps around in flashback and uses many different points of view.

Modern fans name another filmmaker as the best American writer and director of our time. George Lucas is best known for creating the *Star Wars* saga. Before the *Star Wars* trilogy, Lucas also made *American Graffiti*, a slice of life story about California teenagers growing up in the rock-and-roll era. *American Graffiti* is still one of the most profitable films of all time and has rated highly on many lists of the best films.

A Look at Foreign Masters

Foreign films have a limited audience in the U.S.; the idea of reading subtitles at a movie is not appealing to some people. Foreign films might seem complicated or too boring for you, but they will help you appreciate the view American directors take as opposed to the approaches preferred in other parts of the world.

Foreign masters are responsible for some landmark films that affected cinema in many ways. The largest competitors to Hollywood are the massive industries of India and Nigeria, though their studio models and distribution channels are different from those used in the U.S.

The French New Wave

One of the most influential movements within film was the French New Wave. Out of disgust for the conventional structure and story lines offered up by traditional French cinema, the idea of making more original pieces grew. A group of French filmmakers, led by François Truffaut, Jean-Luc Godard, and Jacques Demy in the 1950s and '60s, embraced this by rejecting traditional cinematic structure and told more personal stories. These films were produced at a low cost, using simple techniques and ordinary locations. The idea beyond these films was to shock the viewer with unexpected camera work and disjointed editing. Many of these movies used the auteur style and told a form of the filmmaker's life story or a deeply personal story. A classic example of this style is *The 400 Blows*, François Traffaut's tale of a troubled adolescence. Antoine, a well-meaning boy in a family troubled by infidelity, is rejected by his parents. Truffaut has said the story has roots in his own family life.

Japanese cinema

Japan has a longstanding and celebrated tradition of cinema. Japanese cinema has been celebrated as better than other Asian cinema, and the 1950s are considered the Golden Age of Japanese cinema. During this time *Seven Samurai*, a highly influential Japanese film, was released. Writer and director Akira Kurosawa is credited with the first use of many now conventional plot devices in this film. The story is about seven samurai hired by a village to protect their crops and exposes the difficulty between the two classes of people in Japanese society back in the 1500s.

Japanese horror films gained more of a cult following in America in the 2000s. As many Japanese horror films were remade in English, American audiences started wanting to see the originals that pushed the envelope. An example is *Ringu*, the original on which Hollywood remake *The Ring* starring Naomi Watts was made.

The size and scope of Bollywood

The cinema industry of India rivals Hollywood in its size and cash-earning power. Bollywood movies are characterized by musical numbers, which in older films seemed nonsensical and unrelated to the plot line. The music is as big an industry as the films themselves, with the songs from a movie released to the public before the movie is. This allows the anticipation to build surrounding the movie, and often how good the music is impacts the film's box office. Modern Bollywood films feature exotic locales, such as Miami and France, and tell complicated stories that span different genres, most often surrounding love and marriage. Indian audiences expect a little of everything, a roller coaster ride of emotions. In keeping with India's stricter family values, the hero and heroine are seen sharing a kiss and nothing more, though some films have pushed the line on this with mixed results.

Bollywood films can push three-hour running times and are shown with an intermission at the Indian cinema. Scenes or concepts from popular American films, such as *Pretty Woman*, have been remade to be more palatable for Indian audiences. In *Chori Chori Chupke Chupke*, a couple troubled with infertility hires a prostitute to act as a surrogate for a baby they will pass off as their own. Bollywood films have followings in many countries besides India, as people of Indian descent and Westerners who like the lush visuals and unusual music watch them in Canada, the UK, and the Middle East.

The advance of Nollywood

Nollywood, the nickname given to Nigeria's booming film industry, currently produces the second most films in any given year, with Bollywood coming in first and the U.S. third. In the last 20 years, cinema in Nigeria has become more popular and prolific. The films are shot in English, and the industry itself has changed Nigeria's economy by bringing in more money and employing a large number of Nigerians. The films are produced quickly and cheaply without the kinds of luxuries a Hollywood film offers. The movies then are distributed on video or disc instead of directly to the theater the way Hollywood and Bollywood movies are. As westerners grow more interested in these films, documentaries are being made about the industry.

Where to find classic and foreign films

Now that video stores are almost obsolete, people who want to watch something besides the latest mainstream new releases have to look harder.

- Online: The Criterion Collection streams online via Hulu® Plus as part of a monthly subscription fee. Hulu Plus offers a free one-month trial for students and a standard one-week trial for anyone. Movies include *Seven Samurai, The 400 Blows,* and *Harlan County USA*. Netflix® also offers some classic movies through its Qwikster online streaming service and more through its DVD mail service.

- Specialty Channels: Turner Classic Movies shows movies from the 1930s on with limited commercials, and they are uncut from their original form. The IFC and Sundance® channels often show acclaimed foreign films.

If you find that you really enjoy foreign films, you can put elements from them in your screenplay. *Moulin Rouge* draws influence from traditional Hollywood musicals but also has Bollywood influences. The musical number at the climax of the film even has a dancer with the head of an elephant, commonly associated with the Hindu god Ganesh.

Developing a
Story Concept

*H*aving learned a little about the industry, the business, and how scripts are sold, now you can turn your attention to yourself and your new screenplay. The first step is turning your idea into a whole story concept.

The actual idea, the light bulb moment that gives you the idea so compelling you are sure it is a hit, can come from anywhere. That seed of an idea has to be expanded and turned into a concept that can sustain a whole movie.

Once you begin writing a screenplay, you will find new ideas come to you from everywhere. They might be questions, such as what is it like to be an Alaskan fisherman, or what is it like for an average person to marry a Hollywood celebrity. Sometimes questions can be combined to make a stronger premise. Perhaps your Alaskan fisherman is the one to marry a Hollywood star. The complications are inherent: He does not fit in with her Hollywood friends; she does not fit in with his hardworking, conservative family. So far, we have an idea, but it has too many clichés in the premise because we have little detail about our story. This is where you must dig deeper into the idea to get to the specifics.

What is Your Movie About?

The first step toward deciding what your movie is about is creating the logline. The logline is a term for a one-sentence synopsis of your movie. It seems impossible, and yet it has been done for every movie in existence. Consider:

- *Knocked Up* — A type-A reporter has a one-night stand with a loveable slacker and ends up pregnant.

- *The Fighter* — A down-on-his-luck boxer tries to mount a comeback to help his drug-addicted brother.

Your logline should summarize the story idea and offer a hook to pique interest. To create a logline, you have to spend some time considering the other major parts of your movie. Who is the movie about? What do they want? What are they going to do to get it? Who wants to stop them from getting it? These questions will help you begin to decide what action will take place to propel your story from beginning to end.

Keep this logline visible as you write your script. How you do this is up to you. Put it on a sticky note on your mirror, post it on the fridge with a magnet, have it scroll across your computer screen as the screen saver. The idea is to keep the logline in view and fresh in your mind. If you find yourself stuck in a scene or not sure what comes next, focus on the logline.

Your movie is about someone who wants something because that is what all screenplays at their core are about. Your character has a need or a problem that needs to get fixed. To keep your audience interested, your character has to be willing to go out and do something about this problem. Maybe this is his or her character. Maybe it is completely out of left field, a first-time occurrence. No matter what, your main character has to go out and take charge of his or her destiny. No one wants to watch someone sit around and wait for things to happen. In *Something Borrowed*, Rachel accidentally sleeps with her lifelong best friend's fiancé before the wedding. Despite her best friend, Darcy, being a self-centered princess, Rachel doubts whether Dexter, the guy who has charmed both friends, will choose her over the more demanding Darcy. The film then loses steam as Rachel sits around and waits to see if Dexter will choose to be with her. She finally gathers her nerve and asks Dexter straight out if they have a future together, but the film fails to build enough energy in the remaining time.

In every movie there has to be a central problem. This ties directly to what your character wants. To use an obvious example, in *Harold and Kumar Go to White Castle*, what the protagonists want is to go to White Castle. The problem is that White Castle is no longer where it used to be. Usually, as the movie progresses, the central problem spirals into several problems. Once you decide on your main character's problem, examine it to see if it is urgent. If there is a time crunch, that is even better. It automatically gives the movie a sense of urgency. In *The Hangover*, the groomsmen only have hours to find their missing friend and deliver him to his wedding.

Choosing a genre for your screenplay

At some point throughout this process, you will have to choose a genre for your work. You might find this difficult. Many movies span more than one genre, but you will have to choose the one that represents your work the best.

For example, look at the movie *The Blind Side*. The journey of Michael Oher, who starts the movie sleeping on the streets and winds up being drafted to the NFL, is a moving drama. The way he gets there, through the love and acceptance of the Tuohy family, is a feel-good family story. There are scenes between Michael and his new younger brother, SJ, that make the viewer laugh as hard as any comedy and football scenes that would fit in a sports movie. However, at its core, *The Blind Side* is still a drama.

When you try to sell the movie, one of the first questions you will be asked is what category it fits into. This is important to the film's marketing. Many sub-genres exist within each genre. Some genres that exist are:

- **Action** — Movies that center around action, fighting, or martial arts. Some examples of this genre are *Die Hard, The Transporter,* and any Jackie Chan film.

- **Comedy** — Movies that seek to make us laugh, even if they also tell another story. Some examples of this genre are *Knocked Up, Bad Teacher,* and *Tootsie*.

- **Drama** — Emotional stories that take the viewer on a journey. Some examples of this genre are *Terms Of Endearment, Seabiscuit,* and *The King's Speech*.

- **Family** — Movies the whole family can enjoy together. Family is another genre that many other genres creep into. Many family comedies exist, such as *Freaky Friday*. But everything from animated features such as *Shrek* and *The Lion King* to live action movies like *Spy Kids* and *The Sisterhood of the Traveling Pants* fall into the family genre.

- **Horror** — Movies designed to scare and delight, whether through heavy suspense or on-screen gore, such as *Paranormal Activity*, *The Hills Have Eyes*, or *The Shining*.

- **Romance** — Sentimental stories such as *Up Close and Personal*, but also romantic comedies like *The Proposal*.

- **Biography** — Movies that tell the story of someone's life. These can range from stories of famous entertainers, such as *Walk The Line* or *What's Love Got To Do With It*, to movies about regular people with extraordinary lives, like *Erin Brockovich*.

- **Science fiction** — Modern-day creature features like *Cloverfield*, apocalypse movies such as *2012*, and alien movies like *Independence Day*, all fall into this genre.

Setting your idea apart

In Hollywood, everything old is constantly new again. Remakes are always plentiful, with *Planet of The Apes*, *Footloose*, and *Charlie's Angels* all remade in 2011. Old ideas often have a new spin, like the classic story of Beauty and the Beast being repurposed into 2011's *Beastly*. Sometimes it seems the same idea gets passed around, such as when *No Strings Attached* and *Friends With Benefits* came out within weeks of each other. It is not surprising to see why a screenwriter could think Hollywood does not want new, original ideas.

What they are looking for is the same old thing but newer. Any idea that has a built-in audience is an easier sell than something new and outside the box. This is why remakes seem to be constantly emerging, even as audiences bemoan the lack of originality. Though we might say we do not want to see the same thing over again, something appeals to us about a remake. Sometimes it is the nostalgia of seeing an old favorite on the big screen, like *Fame, The Smurfs,* or *Spiderman.* Sometimes it is just a sure bet. Rather than risk your ever-increasing price of admission on something you have never heard of, maybe it is better to go with something you know will end happily or that you know will be appropriate for your kids. If you plunk down your hard-earned dollar for *Wall Street: Money Never Sleeps,* you can assume it will follow the same lines as the first one: Man enters the stock market, learns greed is good, gets in way over his head. The details that have changed will be just enough of a surprise to keep you interested.

Rather than deny or let this human tendency to like the familiar irritate you, use it to your advantage. Your idea is bound to be similar to something that has come before. To keep it interesting, you have to find a way to infuse a new energy, a fresh perspective on this situation. Making your characters unlike the ones that have come before is one way to do this. Perhaps you can take something you are passionate about and use it to make your characters unique. If you practice meditation, maybe one of your characters does, too. The way you speak might be unique enough to add some flavor to your script. *Juno* told the story of an unexpected pregnancy, not an unusual circumstance. But by keeping the language true to today's teen, the movie becomes more comedic and sweet in tone. Maybe your children provide the comic relief in your life. Your protagonist's children can do the same in your screenplay. Find ways to add these personal touches, the things that make the script unique and truly you.

Researching Your Idea

Once you have come up with the idea you will turn into a screenplay, it is time to conduct research. This research is different from the research you conducted into screenwriting. This time, the subject of your research will depend on what your screenplay is about. It is up to you to analyze the idea you have in mind. What parts of the story are you not familiar with? Research to learn more about these parts.

Location

Much ties into the location of a story. You have to learn about the actual physical location; you can study maps about the place and read up on the history of the place online. But if you hope you capture the mentality of the people who live there, you might want to visit that area. For example, the animators and writers researching *Cars* drove along historic Route 66 to study and learn the effects of development on the small towns along the way.

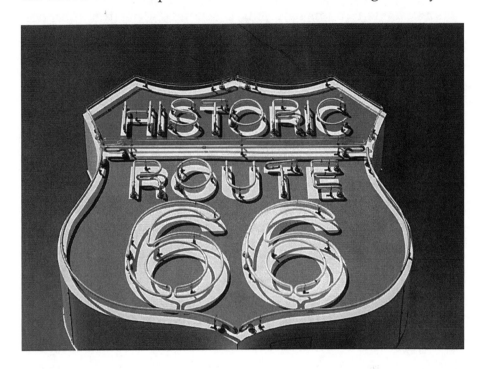

Language

The dialect spoken by people in a particular area can be distinctive. Even if the people do not speak in a particular dialect, slang words and colloquialisms might be more popular in that area. Different words can be considered vulgar in different countries or contexts. The word bloody, though not often used in the U.S., is not seen as a curse, while it is in the UK.

The movie *Mean Girls* skewers this effectively as Gretchen Weiners, one of the popular girls, is seen throughout the movie using the word "fetch" to mean something that is cool. The slang, she explains, comes from England. By using it, Gretchen hopes to appear hip and ahead of the other kids. But the word never catches on, no matter how hard Gretchen tries. In the end, when queen mean girl Regina George tells her to stop trying so hard to make "fetch" cool, it is only a second before the audience, exasperated with the word as well, snaps. In the overall story, it serves as a plot point in the impending end of Gretchen and Regina's friendship. All of this is built out of one word that does not quite fit with the teen slang.

In the film *Hustle and Flow*, use of the right slang gives the film its authenticity. DJ, the Memphis pimp at the center of the story, would not be as believable if he spoke in perfect school English. For the movie *Clueless*, writer Amy Heckerling did not want her characters' Valley Girl slang to sound outdated, so she made up many of the words. Some viewers still criticized the dialogue as out of date.

Occupation

You might think your character has no occupation to research. But even those who do not necessarily collect a paycheck have a job within the family and an important role to play within the dynamic of your script. If there are kids in your script, it is your job to determine what those kids like to do. You remember when you were a child and the things you liked to do. But times are changing, and the games that are essential to one generation's memories are obsolete by the time a new generation comes along. If you are not raising kids or grandkids, you might be surprised by how advanced some of the popular games for today's kids are. One simple example is the virtual reader, a toy that is essentially a junior version of an adult's Amazon Kindle. Children can use this toy to read to them, thereby eliminating the need for mom and dad to read with them. Unlike in past times, the children can be put in the minivan, a movie turned on, and headphones placed over their ears. The games invented out of necessity 20 years ago, games such as License Plate Bingo and I Spy, are nonexistent in some homes. It is up to you, as the writer, to determine whether this is a tragedy that shows how deeply American family values have deteriorates or a sanity-saving miracle.

Choosing a secretive or unknown profession can add another dimension to your movie. In *Duplicity*, Julia Roberts and Clive Owen begin the story as government spies in Dubai. This is a job we have seen in countless movies, so the audience does not need much explanation of Claire's work for the American government or Ray's job as an MI6 agent. But in the next scene, both have left the service of their respective governments and moved to the world of corporate espionage, a world most of the movie-going public does not even know exists. Though this is a new world for the viewer, we understand that the stakes are high.

Time period

Period movies require more research than movies set in our time. Even those who conduct diligent research sometimes can face criticism and backlash. The novel *Memoirs of a Geisha*, which the author researched extensively, became controversial after it was published and made into a movie. One of the women cited as a source on geisha life claimed the author had breached her trust and that his portrayal was not accurate. Though a movie is a work of fiction and it does come out of your imagination, if it is shown to be patently untrue, the viewer can be turned off. The defense that it is a work of fiction and not meant to be historically accurate does not stand up to scrutiny. The movie *10,000 BC* was criticized heavily for being inaccurate to the period. The story itself concerned D'Leh, a tribesman who crosses the treacherous ancient world to recapture his love, Evolet. Among the chief criticisms leveled at the film were:

- The main actors spoke in English, while other clans they met spoke different dialects or made up languages. Scholars agree that English did not exist in 10,000 BC.

- Animals resembling dinosaurs and giant birds appear at points in the film. Dinosaurs were extinct by 10,000 BC, as were the large birds of prehistory.

- The humans in the society D'Leh finds at the end of the movie seem to be working together as a team to create the pyramids. Most humans at this time lived nomadically. Though they are not named Egyptians, they are acting a great deal like the Egyptians; only they are working on a project the Egyptians had not built yet. The pyramids and Sphinx were not yet created.

- The people in the Egyptian-style society D'Leh finds worship a leader known as the Almighty. However, during that historical period, the people were more likely to worship a sun god than a human on Earth.

- Weapons that were not created until much later were used in the film's battles. Animals were portrayed as being under the control of humans, which did not occur until later in history. At that point in history, man was still working on using inanimate objects to get to a further goal, like using gourds to carry water.

The film's director, Roland Emmerich, later went on to say that he meant this film to be a representation of a lost society. Defenders of the film also have pointed out reasons the creative decisions were made. For example, though English was perhaps not invented yet, neither was any other language currently in existence. Fans of the film defended the choice of English by saying it made the most sense to the viewing audience, even if it was not historically correct. Emmerich also has said he chose to make the movie in English so the audience could get emotionally involved. As an established and successful director by the time he made this film, Emmerich had the leeway to make creative decisions like this. The same courtesy is not generally extended to a first-time screenwriter. A reader who goes over a script from a first-time writer that does not seem accurate will most likely toss it aside.

Research tools

There are a few tried and true ways to research a topic:

- **Books:** Look hard enough, and you can find books on any topic. Conducting research via books can be expensive if you run to the local mall and buy every one. Keep your costs low by checking for eBooks or picking up at the library, flea market, secondhand store, yard sales, or discount websites such as half.com® (**www.half.ebay.com**).

- **Interviews:** Knock on doors; make phone calls; ask away. Your own nervousness or shyness will be your biggest hindrance. Find subjects by searching online, networking through friends, and making cold calls. Enlist help when you can. Try asking friends, co-workers, or family members if they know anyone with knowledge about your subject. Call the PR office of your local community college or vocational school and see if they can recommend a professor who has some knowledge of your topic. People like to talk about themselves and will be happy to answer your questions. Once the person has granted you the interview, try to be courteous. Arrive on time, or call on time, and be prepared with your questions. If you have access to a tape recorder or digital recorder, bring this along, as it will save you scrambling to take notes.

- **Movies:** Other movies doubtlessly exist about the same topic. Although some people avoid taking in other forms of media, as they fear it will influence their creativity, reading what already exists on the subject is the best way to avoid duplicating it. One of the reasons you cannot copyright an idea is because any idea can occur to multiple people at the same time.

- **Fact-finding trips:** Taking a trip to scout a location sounds like a high-cost endeavor, something only established writers have money to do. But you might be able to find something local that will assist you in your work. For example, if you want to craft a period piece set in Spain, traveling to Spain might be way outside your budget. But many examples of Spanish architecture exist in Florida and California, and even in Minnesota, there is a house created in the style of the famous Alhambra palace in Spain.

Once you have conducted research to make sure your idea is viable, re-examine your story idea. Will it still work given the historical constraints? Does it make sense for your main character, a doctor, to offer unsolicited medical advice to homeless people on the subway all the while knowing it opens him up to legal liability? Maybe you decide this is part of his attitude. Though the danger of legal action is there, he takes the risk. Maybe this shows his character as a maverick that does not care about the rules. Maybe he is an optimist who has faith in the true nature of people. Maybe it shows him to be arrogant, convinced he will never make a misdiagnosis.

How Characters Shape Your Idea

If you are still lost within your story concept, getting to know your characters better can help. Determining what kind of background they have will help you decide how they view the world. Deciding what experiences they had in the past can help you figure out how they will deal with the problems they encounter in your story.

Let's say the Alaskan fisherman from the earlier example gets the Hollywood starlet pregnant. Naturally, we would expect him to propose marriage, based on his conservative background, and her to smile sadly as she tells him she will be having an abortion and does not want to see him anymore. But perhaps in this version, when he drops to his knee, she reveals that she also had a conservative upbringing and ran away from home to follow her dreams. She always wanted to go home to see her parents again but never had the nerve. Now, with him as her husband, she can hope to reunite with them. This scenario is one way her background could turn the story. There are others: Perhaps he proposes, she accepts, and they elope to Las Vegas. They return to her mansion and await the baby. But he feels uncomfortable in her fancy beach house and uneasy without work to fill his days. His father was a no-good layabout who drank himself to death. His horror at the thought of meeting the same end is what always motivated him. Now his background has come into play as well.

Knowing the specifics about your characters will help you know what works for your story. Take the time to get to know each of them and, most important, what each wants over the course of your screenplay.

Creating believable characters

The best way to show your audience who your characters are begins with your knowing who they are. Then you have to reveal this to the audience in a way they will find believable. You cannot force character description into dialogue because it sounds fake.

JAKE
You know, Mike, you're my best friend. Ever since I
got home from Iraq, where I spent four hard years,
me and my wife just haven't been the same.

No one talks to a best friend like that. Remember that your dialogue has to be convincing. A better way to say the above would be in an exchange between Jake and Mike.

MIKE
How have things been since you got home?

JAKE
Good, I suppose. Glad to see my kids. Damn happy
my Harley's still running after four years in the
garage.

MIKE
What about Laura?

JAKE
Laura doesn't say much.

More about writing convincing dialogue will be covered in Chapter 9.

Though what your characters say is important, the thing that will convince the audience of the nature of your characters is the way they act. In the above scene, Mike comes off as a concerned friend. The things he says are the correct responses. But if he excuses himself to use the bathroom and then kisses Laura passionately in the kitchen, the audience will be convinced he is a dirty scumbag and nothing he says again will change their minds. He will have to show a pattern of change in his behavior to redeem himself in the viewer's eye.

The characters you need

You will need a few characters in your script. Each of these characters serves a purpose. Together, they keep your story moving, and the conflicts between them will advance the plot.

The Protagonist

Every story centers on a protagonist, the person the movie is about. The screenplay follows the protagonist's journey to get what he or she wants. This is true even if he or she does not have the most screen time. The audience does not have to like your protagonist, but they do have to be interested in him or her, and it does help if they can relate to what this character is going through.

The Likability Factor

Can an unlikable person be the protagonist at the center of a likeable movie? Yes, but typically only if they become more tolerable as the film progresses. In *About A Boy*, Hugh Grant's character began as a lonely man. As the story progressed, he became more likeable as he opened up his life. In the screenwriting guide *Save The Cat*, author Blake Snyder advises screenwriters to take a moment early on in the screenplay to make the character likeable. The character should save a cat or show some other unexpected kindness. This serves to convince the audience of his inherent likability and help them relate to him.

The Reluctant Protagonist

A reluctant protagonist is different from a passive one. Some screenwriting experts say that Cameron, Ferris Bueller's best friend in *Ferris Bueller's Day Off* is the true protagonist of the story. As the movie progresses, Ferris does not have much of an arc and does not change much. But Cameron changes; he learns to stand up to his overbearing father.

The Antagonist

The antagonist is the person whose desires most clash with the protagonist's. Perhaps his or her aim is to stop the protagonist, or perhaps he or she desires a different outcome than the one the protagonist does. Let's say your protagonist is hoping for a big promotion at work. If your antagonist hopes to stop the protagonist at any cost, he or she would act differently than an honest, hardworking antagonist who hopes to win the same promotion. The obstacles that stand in the way of your hero getting his or her goal are what make the movie interesting. Much of this will come from your antagonist and how he or she attempts to stop the protagonist. Think of the classic character played by Tommy Lee Jones in *The Fugitive*, chasing endlessly after Harrison Ford. His conviction that he was chasing a criminal kept him motivated. Tom Hanks played a similar character in *Catch Me If You Can*, a police officer who chased Leonardo DiCaprio across the globe. Both of these movies feature an antagonist who chases the protagonist. Both antagonists have moments where they doubt their mission.

An antagonist who is mean-spirited, evil, or plays dirty can come off to the audience as unrealistic unless his or her motivations are explained. The antagonist simply being "crazy" or "evil" is not enough of a reason. In *Cars*, Lightning McQueen's nemesis, Chick Hicks, fights dirty, a fact the writers set up within the first few minutes of the film. Over the course of the movie, we learn that Chick has been a perpetual runner-up to another racer, Strip "The King" Weathers. In the race that takes place at the end of the film, Chick purposely runs into The King, sending him flying. The audience accepts that Chick would do this, not because he has gone crazy, but because he is tired of losing.

The Reflection

The reflection is the best friend, the character the protagonist can turn to in a bind and spill his or her deepest secrets. The reflection also can serve as the voice of reason by reminding the protagonist why his or her actions are out of line. In this way, the reflection can act as the voice of the audience and air the skepticisms they might have at the same time. In *My Best Friend's Wedding*, this is Rupert Everett calmly asking Julia Roberts who is chasing her as she chases the groom. When she says no one, he points out that this is her answer. Though she does not listen to him, the audience is satisfied. If your protagonist is going to be wrapped up in wacky hijinks, having a reflection that does not hold his or her tongue is essential. It saves your viewers from having to exit the theater grumbling about how in real life someone would have told her to stop. The reflection character also can help the protagonist advance his or her desire, help them devise a course of action, or help enact whatever plan he or she has.

The Romance Character

If you have decided that your movie does not need a love story, that is fine. A movie can succeed without a love story in the background. However, a love story often factors well into a movie, especially if the movie tells a coming-of-age or personal story. In most movies, there is a romance character, a love interest for the protagonist. Often, the protagonist equates capturing this love interest with getting a better life and achieving a goal. Sometimes, the protagonist has to become a better person to attract the love interest. The main character might think that being with this person will make him or her complete. This is not always a romantic interest. In the case of a buddy movie, the romance character simply can be a good friend.

Developing your idea by getting to know your characters

Let's expand a little on the idea about the protagonist who wants a better job. Say her name is Emma, and she works in a grocery store. She wants to move up to manager so she can make more money and have a better life. Unfortunately for her, Jackie, her perfectly punctual co-worker, also wants the promotion. This is a basic idea. To get to the events that will take place in the script, we need more specific details about our protagonist and antagonist.

Emma wants a better life, which is a good start. But what specifically does she want? To own her own home and get out of her overbearing mother's grasp? Maybe she wants to move out of her hometown, where she feels stifled, and start fresh somewhere new. Even this idea is not specific enough. Where is the hometown? Where does she hope to move? Is she headed for a big city on the same coast or across the country? Why has she chosen this place? Creating a fictional city to set the movie in allows you the freedom to create all the specifics. Let's say she lives in the small town of Grossville, and the movie's working title is *Getting Out of Grossville*.

And what about the reflection? Emma's friend, Elaine, also works at the grocery store but in a different department. She also wants to save money to move away, but she would rather do it in a different way, without going after this promotion. Maybe it is another job, maybe it is a dumb boyfriend she is milking for money, and maybe she is stealing meat out of the deli freezer and selling it to people. The point is that she can be Emma's support system with no conflict of interest. Maybe at one point down the line, Emma has an interview for the promotion and panics and seriously embellishes on her résumé and experience. Elaine can help her practice answers to the questions that make her sound more qualified. Or maybe Elaine can cover for Emma's absence at work when Emma is too busy with the romance character. The point is, these two are friends until the end.

The classic example of this is Cyn, the Joan Cusack character in *Working Girl*. As Melanie Griffith's Tess fakes her way to the top, her best friend Cyn helps her but also tries to warn her of the mistakes she is making. Cyn pretends to be Tess' secretary, so Tess can pretend to be a broker in her boss's absence. But Cyn also tells Tess when she starts to go down the wrong path. In the movie *Maid In Manhattan*, Jennifer Lopez's character never would be able to impersonate a rich hotel guest without the help of her friends, who distract the real rich guest and offer Lopez access to her fabulous outfits.

Chapter 4

Adapting an Existing Work

any people feel they have lived lives worth retelling, and some of these people are right. Rather than work from a completely original idea, you can choose to adapt an existing work, such as a book, a stage play, or the story of someone's life. Adaptation is a different from writing an original script, as a larger portion of your time might be taken up with research, conducting interviews, reviewing source material, and collaborating with the person who inspired or wrote the original work.

Who hasn't read a book, then went to see the movie and thought the book was much better? Not every story that works on the page is destined for the screen. Novels are much longer than books and allow the author to spend pages explaining the inner thoughts and feelings of the characters. Screenwriters do not get quite so much. Instead of explaining with words, they have to show the audience the way the characters are feeling by the things that they do and the way they interact with each other.

For a first-time writer, adapting a work like a biography can be challenging, as the events of a person's life do not necessarily conform well to the structure of a screenplay. You might need to focus on a section of a person's life to make the story better. Screenwriters often have to exclude parts of the story or embellish certain parts to make it more interesting. The movie *The Perfect Storm* was based on a book about the true events that took place in 1991 to the real crew of the Andrea Gail. The writers in that case were later sued for adding fictionalized details to the lives of certain fishermen. The family of the captain of the ship sued the studio that produced the movie because they said he was shown as unprofessional. The case went all the way to the Florida Supreme Court and was then lost. This is just one example of how taking artistic license with a story based on someone's life can be a risk. Even though the people or the estate might initially agree, they might not like the way they are portrayed in your script and change their minds about their involvement. If you do speak with the person who created the original work, be careful about committing to portray him or her in a certain light. Until you begin the research and writing, you do not know what turns the story might take.

Adapting Another Source Material

Screenwriting is a creative expression. Any art form might inspire you to think up your story. A good song can tell a story in four minutes. A good poem can paint a new world for you to see in your imagination. Some examples of unusual sources that have been turned into feature films are:

- *Julie and Julia* is the story of the life of Julia Child, the renowned chef and author. It is also the story of Julie Powell, a New Yorker who writes a blog about her attempt to cook every recipe in Child's recipe book, *Mastering the Art of French Cooking*, in a year. The source material for the parts about Child's life is her autobiography. Powell also wrote a memoir about her experience writing the blog, *Julie and Julia: 365 Days, 524 Recipes, 1 Tiny Apartment Kitchen*, and the film was adapted from this book. The movie is now said to be the first adapted from a blog.

- Johannes Vermeer's painting *Girl with a Pearl Earring* inspired the book and movie of the same name. The movie, which was released in 2003, tips its hat to the painting by using the same colors that appear in the painting in its cinematography, richly recreating 17th century Holland. Little was known about the circumstance under which the portrait was painted, so the screenwriters had to create the story using the few facts known about Vermeer and the customs and rituals of the period. In the movie, Scarlett Johansson plays Griet, a servant in the painter's household who serves as both a model and a sort of apprentice to the painter. As Vermeer's wife grows more suspicious and resentful, Griet learns from the master, who hopes to keep her away from his patron, a man of loose morals. Eventually, Griet poses for the portrait wearing the pearl earrings that belong to the painter's wife.

- People's experiences are the basis of movies by way of their book adaptations. Danny Wallace's book *Yes Man* inspired the movie of the same name, starring Jim Carrey as a man who says yes to every offer that comes his way. In real life, Wallace said yes to all kinds of things for a year, after a stranger on a bus suggested he start saying yes more. In another example, the website **http://SaveKaryn.com** was Karyn Bosnak's way to attempt to get herself out of exorbitant credit card debt by soliciting help from strangers over the Internet. In the early 2000s, when the Internet was relatively new to most people, this idea had some novelty and was featured on the national news, which enabled Karyn to reach her goals. The story was optioned for a film, though no date for release has been set.

- The classic board game Battleship was optioned in 2011 to become a feature-length film. *Battleship* was released in 2012 and is the story of the U.S. Navy fighting an alien invasion. In playing the game, players try to sink each other's ships by guessing as to where the opponent's ships are positioned. The movie version will play up this angle, with segments shot from the point of view of either ship, giving the viewer an idea of where they are in relation to each other. The game Clue, which was made into a movie in 1985, will be remade into another film in 2013.

- The hit book, *Go The F**k To Sleep*, was sold as a children's book for adults. The book is a humorous take on parents' struggle to get their babies to sleep, with the look of a children's book, including illustrations and rhyming stanzas. Although it is a simple picture book without much of a story to it, and a title that will make marketing difficult, the film rights have been optioned. The screenwriter charged with adapting the book will have a hard time deciding how to adapt a children's book with profanity and express the thoughts parents are never supposed to say. Turning a short, satirical children's book for adults into a full-length movie could prove difficult. But if done well, an honest and funny look at the harsh realities of parenting could appeal to couples and be a big hit at the box office.

- Many video games have been turned into movies, with varying degrees of success. *The Resident Evil* movie adaptations were successful at the box office and spawned four sequels and another upcoming movie. *Prince of Persia: The Sands of Time* became the most successful video game adaptation of all time.

- Comic books and graphic novels are already visual and often make the leap to the big screen. *Watchmen*, a popular graphic novel about superheroes, took 20 years in development before actually being made. The project was dropped several times by various studios because the material was deemed by some to be too complex. Author of the comic Alan Moore told the press that while he felt the script for the adaptation was well done, he did not intend to see the film. Moore felt his work would not translate into another medium.

- Green Day's concept album *American Idiot* was adapted to a Broadway musical and has been optioned for production as a film. The theme of the album, about a man leaving his suburban town and living in the big city, was expanded in the musical. The characters invented by Green Day for the album were put in the center of the story. However, the musical featured no speaking dialogue and strived to add as little as possible to the existing lyrics. The movie likely will expand on the ideas expressed in the music, of young people rebelling against a sedentary, passive life. ABBA's work went through a similar process of adaptation to create the film *Mamma Mia*. The story first appeared on the stage in London's West End, and then progressed to film.

The Legal Concerns

Before you can turn an existing work into a screenplay, you have to acquire the rights to that work. This can be a fairly straightforward process, or it can be more complicated if multiple people own the work. Any published work is most likely under copyright. The copyright protects the rights of the person who owns or created that work to distribute and copy it. Currently, a copyright protects the work for the writer's life span plus 70 years. This length has changed many times, so works that came out in past years might have a shorter copyright term. After the writer dies, the copyright will protect their estate's interest in the work. Once the copyright expires, the work becomes part of what is called the public domain. Anything that is in the public domain is not protected and is fair game for writers to adapt. If you are interested in finding a work in the public domain, you can look online for lists of available works. Many websites have lists of works in the public domain or even the full text of the work. Project Gutenberg (**www.gutenberg.org**) is a digital library that includes works that are free to adapt. The books are available to view and read online or download to your computer or mobile device. To be sure the work is available to adapt, check the copyright status, found on the bibliographic record tab on the main page of each book listing.

If the work is not in the public domain, contact the copyright owner to see if you can purchase the rights. They already might want to adapt the work themselves or might have sold the work already. They might not want the idea to be adapted into a screenplay because they know the story will be modified. It is best to always look into the copyright before you begin writing, so you do not waste time writing something you will not be able to acquire the rights to.

Getting Around Getting Permission

If you are a new screenwriter with little money but lots of creativity, think about changing your idea. You can begin with the same premise but change details until the story becomes unrecognizable from the story that inspired it. There is nothing wrong with being inspired by another creative work, and no one can sue you for writing your own idea after watching his or hers. After all, you could say Pygmalion inspired everything from *My Fair Lady* to *She's All That*. *Romeo and Juliet* has provided inspiration for everything from *West Side Story* to *Romeo Must Die*. Try changing the idea in the following ways:

- Place the story in a new city. *The Sweet Hereafter* told the story of a small Canadian town rocked by a school bus crash that killed most of the town's children. The story was based on a real-life bus crash in Texas and the subsequent pack of lawyers that descended on the town. The location of the crash was changed in the novel to New York and then to Canada for the film.

- Tell the story from a different perspective. Instead of telling the story from the same narrator as in the inspiring work, change to another person who can provide a different view on the events. *The Last King of Scotland* did this effectively by telling the story of Idi Amin's brutal dictatorship from the view of his latest doctor.

Adapting for Hollywood's Taste

Although you want to be as creative as possible, the ultimate goal is to sell your script to Hollywood. Not every story is suitable for a movie. Keep this in mind as you work on an adaptation. A book that is too technical, that requires too much exposition and explanation for a mainstream audience to understand, might not work as a movie. This was one of the criticisms of the film adaptation of *The Da Vinci Code*. If you choose a source material that has a lot of adult content, that could be the right thing for your script, as long as it has a viable audience.

As you adapt the material, you might have to change or omit some portions to make the story more interesting. You also might have to edit out some material to make the story more palatable to Hollywood. Hollywood prefers a certain kind of ending where disputes are resolved, love is found, and the story is wrapped up neatly. There is a reason for this: Audiences like a happy ending. Although they do not want it to be overly predictable, in the end everyone likes to see the underdog win or love win out in the end. We like to feel the story has been resolved, all the issues more or less wrapped up. Although many films defy these conventions, it can be harder to sell unconventional films, especially for a first-time screenwriter.

What a film does need is a clear and defined audience that will come out to see the movie. If the movie strays too far from the source material, these differences can turn off the built-in audience that comes with it.

Adapting material about controversial subjects

The hit book *The Hunger Games* seemed from the inception a difficult novel to adapt. Set in a grim future, the book chronicles the journey of Katniss Everdeen, who lives in a bleak future where the government forces children to battle to the death, watched by the entire nation. Taken in this manner, the source material seems positively depressing. The idea of children killing each other for the entertainment of society is a hard idea for a Hollywood executive to swallow. In the novel, the things that Katniss enjoys in her simple life — her family, her friend Gale, hunting and running in the woods — balances the horror of the Hunger Games themselves. The reader is able to follow along and root for Katniss, enjoy her triumphs with her. Creating the same kind of connection between the viewer and the character without having young adult viewers dwell too much on the gruesome aspects of the story was a difficult task for the writers of the movie. Yet based on the box office success when it was released in March 2012 — the movie grossed $251 million in ten days — the writers managed to pull together a decent script despite the difficulties.

Though this type of story is new to American screens, a Japanese novel based on a similar concept sparked controversy when it was adapted to a film. In *Battle Royale*, a group of teens are chosen by the government to participate in a "game" of killing. Japanese politicians blamed the film for increases in crimes perpetuated by teenagers. The film was not distributed in North America, and rumors that the U.S. government had banned it helped increase its popularity and sell bootleg copies. Although the film was to be remade for U.S. audiences, the Virginia Tech massacre of 2007 seems to have caused the project to come to a halt.

The classic film *Breakfast at Tiffany's* was changed in many ways from the original inspiration. In the short story by the same name, Holly Golightly was just friends with the nameless narrator. The author, Truman Capote, later said the narrator was gay and could not have held any romantic interest in Holly. For the movie adaptation, the narrator became Paul, and he and Holly fell in love. The end of the movie also was changed to a more conventional happy ending, with Paul and Holly ending up together. The short story had more controversial topics, such as drug use, that were omitted from the movie. Holly Golightly in this version did not indulge in recreational marijuana as she did in the short story. The movie Holly is more of a carefree party girl who is accidentally exposed to dangerous characters instead of someone who is consciously doing wrong. The illegal things she does and the company she keeps are glossed over in the movie.

Other forms of source material are not paced correctly for Hollywood. A large part of adapting material into a screenplay will be choosing events that should stay and those to cut. The bestselling book *The Time Traveler's Wife* was given the big screen treatment in 2009. The source material was nonlinear and jumped around in space and time, which gave the reader the same disoriented feeling as Henry, the time-jumping hero of the story. The book avoided being too confusing because it focused around the true protagonist, Claire. Because a movie about waiting for your husband to come home is not that interesting, the movie had to change somewhat to focus more on the events rather than the feelings between the two.

As a first-time screenwriter, you may find it best to stay away from material you are too attached to that does not fit the Hollywood formula. Even those who have unlimited money to pay have trouble getting their films made sometimes. *The Adventures of Tintin* took 20 years from the purchase of the rights to come to fruition, and that was with as big a name as Steven Spielberg fighting for it. Spielberg bought the options to the Tintin stories back in the 1980s. He commissioned several screenplays before finding a script he liked. Then he had trouble finding the time and funding to make the movie. Tintin, the journalist in the Belgian comic books, is well known throughout Europe and in many countries beyond, to the point where the study of them has its own name: Tintinology. But somehow, the love of Tintin never crossed the pond. Few Americans know the name and fewer still could name any of the secondary characters, such as Tintin's dog Snowy. For the 2011 release, in order to entice North American audiences, it was released in Europe and Asia before the U.S. to build a buzz. Although the film was not the record-breaking success it was in other countries, it has done well at the North American box office.

Modernizing Source Material

There are many possible ways to adapt older source material to make it new and modern. Classic story lines always resonate with audiences. No matter how times change, people always will identify with a story of true love persisting against incredible odds; they never will tire of being taken on a suspenseful ride or waiting for the answer to a good whodunit.

The hit 1998 movie *You've Got Mail* updated the 1940s movie *The Shop Around The Corner*, which was an update of a 1930s play called *Parfumerie*. *You've Got Mail* uses email to update what was always a story about pen pals. At the time the movie was written, email was fairly new and held some novelty with audiences. Both *Parfumerie* and *The Shop Around The Corner* focus on a pair of coworkers at the same shop and have a subplot about the marriage troubles of the shop's owner. *You've Got Mail* gives a modern spin by making Meg Ryan the owner of her own bookstore and Tom Hanks the representative of a large corporation of booksellers. Aspects of the story are still relevant now, more than ten years later. Small independent stores have a harder time making ends meet and are at more risk than ever. And in the age of Facebook and Google, we are more disconnected from one another than ever.

Perhaps no other writer's work has had more adaptations than William Shakespeare. The works of Shakespeare are constantly being adapted into modern ideas. In *Romeo + Juliet*, this Romeo and Juliet live in the present day in a beach town, yet not a word of the dialogue has been updated. In this version, the Montagues and Capulets are heads of industry, their boys running the streets like gangsters. When they cross paths at a gas station, the Montagues and Capulets shoot out their differences instead of crossing swords. Mercutio offers Romeo and the other boys designer drugs before they crash the Capulet party. The movie itself was filmed in a style similar to a music video with bright colors, fast editing, and contemporary music.

Shakespeare's comedies have also been updated. *10 Things I Hate About You* updates *The Taming of The Shrew* and sets it in an American high school where sisters are at opposite ends of the social spectrum. Pretty and popular Bianca rules the school, while people run in fear from the wrath of Kat, the shrew. *Deliver Us From Eva* offered another modern take on *The Taming of the Shrew*. In this version, Eva is the shrew, the only unmarried sister of four. As the oldest sister, she influences the lives of her sisters and causes havoc in their marriages. Fed up, the husbands of the other sisters come together and pay a man to date Eva and keep her too busy to intervene in their lives.

When you try to modernize something, ask the following questions:

- How can new technology change the story? In the day and age we live in, we are all wired to the phone and Internet. In the case of *Romeo and Juliet*, how does Romeo not get the message that Juliet is still alive? Wouldn't she email him, call him, or text him? You can create a plot complication where her father takes her cell phone away or throws it off the balcony into the pool in a rage. Maybe Paris in your adaptation is a tech-savvy stalker type who, Juliet has realized, is monitoring her phone and Internet, so she has to rely on the old-fashioned notion of sending another person with a message. Maybe Romeo sent Juliet a desperate text trying to see if she was really dead, but she had no cell reception in the vault. If you were adapting *Hamlet*, you would have to consider the practical concerns involved in his uncle killing his father: the autopsy, the police investigation. Aren't there surveillance tapes that capture everything that happens at the castle? How does he get away with it, and how is Hamlet the only one who knows? Even the method of murder would need a modern twist, as poison in the ear is a little outdated. Why not think of something more visually stimulating? In Disney's *The Lion King*, the jealous Scar threw his brother King Mufasa off a cliff during a stampede.

- How have society and customs changed? In the original story, Romeo and Juliet were supposed to be teenagers as young as 13 years old. For a modern movie, Romeo and Juliet will have to be older unless they live somewhere where younger marriages are still acceptable. *You've Got Mail* has its two main characters, formerly coworkers, as bookstore owners. In the '40s, it would not have been possible to write the romantic lead of a movie as a single female business owner.

Using an older source material can be beneficial as it might be in the public domain and free for you to use. If you want to try your hand at adaptation, you can try it with a material that you find in the public domain.

Exercise: Updating Little Women

Let's say you were creating a modern *Little Women*, the classic American novel about the four March sisters, Amy, Jo, Beth, and Meg, now a work in the public domain. Tempestuous Jo who was upset she could not fight alongside her father in the Civil War would not be stopped from joining up and being sent to Afghanistan for being a woman. You might have to research other reasons she would be turned down from the service. Maybe she has a medical condition, nothing serious, but enough to keep her home. Perhaps her parents will not allow it, but the minute she turns 18 she signs up behind their back. Maybe the best thing for the story would be to turn the trope on its head: Instead of signing up hoping to get a desk job and being sent into active duty, she signs up hoping to go to war and gets stuck at a desk job. Or maybe after all those years of waiting, Jo is hopeless as part of an infantry unit; she is simply too stubborn and wild at heart. You could take it further and have Jo's quick temper and smart mouth get her sent home from boot camp early, with her mother quick to say, "I told you so." Perhaps this is what prompts the girl's mother to tell Jo she once had a bad temper, too, the way she does in the original novel.

Each sister's story can be modernized in many different ways:

- Beth: Beth's illness might be prolonged by the advanced medical treatment we have now. But the cost of the medical treatments and strain on the family make life even harder for the girl's mother, already struggling to keep things together.

- Amy: In this version, Amy might be a spoiled party girl, coddled by her family into being a brat. Amy might want to get her nose fixed permanently. Perhaps Laurie is a European playboy who embarks on a wild vacation designed to forget Jo with alcohol and other women. Three days later, wandering a strange city high on designer drugs, he crosses paths with Amy and becomes convinced that it is a sign. She will be his salvation.

- Meg: Strangely enough, the easiest story line to modernize might be Meg's story about trying to be accepted into higher strata of society. Though so much time has passed, the disparity between rich and poor in America remains and even grows worse than before.

Exercise: Modernizing the Public Domain

Some simple research will tell you what works are in the public domain. In addition to Project Gutenberg mentioned before, Authorama (**www.authorama.com**) also offers HTML full text versions of classic books that are free for public use. You can choose one you are already familiar with or try a new title. Read it again and try to note details that make the most vibrant pictures.

The short story *Rip Van Winkle* by Washington Irving is a work in the public domain that you might have heard of. The basic idea of a man who sleeps away a portion of his life is fairly well known. The actual story was about a man who lived in an American village, in the Catskill Mountains. The man, whose name was Rip Van Winkle, was a well-loved but lazy man, who wandered away one day with his dog, came across some ghosts, and drank their liquor. He then woke 20 years later to find his children grown and his wife and friends dead. He had missed an entire war.

You could adapt this story in quite a few ways. If you set the story in present day, your protagonist would go to sleep now and wake in the 2030s. Scientists have recently predicted that in the year 2100, we will be controlling our computers via sensors in our brains. Contact lenses wired to the Internet will call up any image or information you wish to see and display it right in front of you. Considering this information, how far along you estimate we will be in 20 years can drastically change the course of your screenplay. Balance this with the knowledge of how far we have come in the last 20 years. In 1992, few people had cell phones, and the ones that did exist were large and expensive. The Internet and home computers in every home were far on the horizon. Everyone did, however, have a Walkman® to play the hottest cassette tapes.

Alternately, your Rip Van Winkle could be waking up in the present day. This could be a way to introduce some nostalgia into the film, in the way that films such as *The Wedding Singer, Hot Tub Time Machine*, and *Definitely, Maybe* have. This could also be a way to tease out the political elements about missing a war. A Van Winkle that wakes up today after 20 years of sleep has missed the events of September 11, the wars in Iraq and Afghanistan, and the conflicts in Libya. He goes to sleep in the middle of a good economy and wakes up in the middle of an economic crisis. He wakes up in the heat of the political race for re-election of the nation's first black president.

There is also this to consider: 20 years in our time, with our current life expectancy, is a fraction of a life. Women are living to 80, men not much less. When the original story was published in 1819, life expectancy was 36 for men and 42 for women. To sleep for 20 years then was to miss half your life. Will your Van Winkle sleep for 40 years to achieve the same effect as the original? Or will he sleep two decades and deal with going from a guy in his early 20s to a man in his middle age who still has the possibility of seeing most his friends and family, albeit a bit older? Either path has interesting possibilities.

How will your Van Winkle get to sleep? Will he drink the alcohol of ghosts as in the original? Or will you update this to a designer drug or a suspended animation, hibernation sleep, such as the one used in the movie *Idiocracy*? Perhaps rather than sleeping, he is in a coma. If you hope to make a film with a political leaning or that hopes to coerce on an issue, here is an opportunity to introduce the issue of living wills and keeping those who are not expected to come back alive.

Society has changed much in these years, and in addition to poking fun at all the gadgets that will shock and awe Rip, chances are the media will take interest in the case of someone who wakes after a long period in a coma or stumbles back to a society after being gone for so long. To make the story credible, his family and the authorities would have tried to look for him as a missing person. Where was Rip that no one found him? Did his family appear on television? Was foul play suspected, and was anyone arrested? In modern society, most people cannot just disappear unnoticed. Maybe that can be a comedic aspect of your script: Rip's family barely noticing he is gone.

By going through the script like this and coming up with ways to modernize the different aspects of the story line, you can retain the familiarity of the original story and the connection or identification that people had with that story. But you are still making the story your own, sculpting and changing it so it is a new tale. You can be as true to the original story as you like, or just take a few aspects of the original and make the rest up yourself. If you are a first time screenwriter, it might help you to have the framework of the original story to reference, with a beginning, middle, and end already laid out for you. The details of how to get to each point are laid out as well. You do not have to take the same route they did, but it does not hurt to have a map.

Developing
Your Characters

*I*n Chapter 2, we went over the characters necessary to the story. Now it is time to sit down and get to know them. Again, the main characters you will need to invent are: the protagonist(s) and the antagonist. Some films, like *Romy and Michele's High School Reunion*, have two protagonists. The antagonist is the person whose wants are most at odds with the protagonist's. In *Mrs. Doubtfire*, the antagonist is Stuart Dunmire, the man who dates Robin Williams' wife. He or she might be evil or might just be a regular person who gets caught up in the moment.

The Flipside

Some hit books have been written telling the other side of popular tales. *Wicked*, the book that spawned the popular musical, tells the story of events preceding the classic *The Wizard of Oz*. The story, told from the perspective of the wicked witch, documents how Glenda the good witch and The Wicked Witch of the West become enemies and fight over the Land of Oz. The book is one of a series that retells the happenings in Oz from a different perspective. *The Three Little Pigs* has received the same treatment by making the wolf the victim in the book, *The True Story of the 3 Little Pigs*. To have an interesting take on an old tale, try to envision your story from the antagonist's perspective.

Other characters are the romance character and the reflection. In the typical Hollywood ending, the protagonist would end up with the romance character, but this is not always the case. The reflection is the best friend, the shoulder that your protagonist can always cry on, the port in a storm. The reflection character in *Legally Blonde* is Paulette, the manicurist that Elle befriends after going to Harvard.

The Truth Hurts

Married couples do it. Best friends do it. Parents and children do it. Everybody fights. You should not shy away from confrontation between your protagonist and your reflection. If your reflection truly is a best friend to your protagonist, it is his or her job as a friend to raise an alarm when the protagonist acts out of character or gambles with his or her life. How can you as the writer keep this scene from seeming clichéd? Try to be specific as to what about the protagonist's action is bothering the friend. Instead of having the reflection say "you've changed" or "you're a different person now," have him or her say exactly what is different. In *The Devil Wears Prada*, when Andy's best friend Lily confronts her about how much she has changed, she does not make a generic statement. She points out how this Andy is different from the Andy she has always known.

And we can add the secondary characters. In sports movies, they are the other players on the team; in family movies, they are the crazy aunts and uncles that fill the background of the barbecue or family reunion. The other fraternity brothers in *Old School*, the other kids that make up Jack Black's class in *School Of Rock*, these are the secondary characters that can make the comedy relief and real-life scenarios that will get your screenplay notice. *More on making these characters memorable later in this chapter.*

Once you have decided on these characters, it is time to learn a little more about them. This is time for you to build these characters from the ground up. Creating a personality and history for your characters will help you make them real. Coming up with the background, and documenting it before you begin writing, will help you keep your characters distinct. Not all of this background will make it into the final movie, nor should it. The backstory informs you as the writer, and you can use it to illuminate some of the characters' motivations for the audience.

How far you need to delve into each character's background is up to you, and it will vary from character to character. You will need more for your protagonist, as he or she is the most important person in the story. Developing too much backstory can turn into time wasted for you if it is not useful.

Before asking a friend for a favor, chances are you will consider how he or she handled it last time. After all, if he or she were sour and made you feel guilty for asking, chances are you will not ask again. The same is true for your secondary characters. The experiences they have are what they will base their decisions on. Knowing that your character has turmoil in his or her past does not mean he or she cannot change over the course of the movie. Audiences can be skeptical and cynical, but we as people like to believe in the better nature of others.

Important Parts of Your Characters' Histories

The histories of your characters dictate many aspects about them. Deciding on a few key elements before you begin to write will help you make them more authentic and more distinct from the other characters.

Hometown

Where your characters are from affects everything from the way they talk to the values they have. Where they live now also says much about them. If they live in different places then where they were born, why did they leave? Were they running from something? Are they looking for new starts? In 2008's *The Visitor*, Walter Vale, a lonely widower, discovers an immigrant couple living in his Manhattan apartment. A con artist who claims the place is his has taken them in. Knowing they have nowhere to go and because he has the extra room, Walter decides to let them stay and begins a friendship with them. Walter learns later on that they are illegally in the United States and are trying to make a better life. The reader has to know why they have come to be there. The customs and culture of their past also come into play.

Family

Your parents shape you as an individual. Knowing the parents of your characters is as important as knowing the characters themselves. Are they strict or freethinking hippies? Was your character raised in a religious home? The things that happen in our childhoods influence our behaviors as adults.

In *The Kids Are All Right*, Joni and Laser deal well with having two moms. Their moms, Nic and Jules, are a pair of opposites who seem to balance each other out. Nic and Jules each got pregnant and had a baby, using sperm from the same donor. Nic is the stricter parent and takes more of a disciplinarian role, while Jules is more relaxed with a more creative spirit. Everything is going fine until Paul, the sperm donor, shows up and starts sleeping with Jules. How the children react to this development reflects the influence the moms have had on them. Each reacts more like their birth mother. Finding out about the affair leads Joni to cut Paul completely out of her life. We see the stern face and strict morals of her birth mother, Nic, coming through in her personality here. Her brother responds more like his birth mom Jules, with a shade of forgiveness and a softer heart.

Culture

The cultural expectations of family can be difficult for a person to buck. As more and more immigrant families populate America, the children of these families struggle with being first generation Americans. But fighting culture can also mean fighting the status quo in your family or town. Being the first in a family to go to college or the first to leave your hometown can alienate the people you love most.

In *My Big Fat Greek Wedding*, protagonist Toula wants to fight against her culture. Toula wants to experience the world and be in charge of her own life, but her traditional Greek parents do not see the need.

Age

When they were born and the generation they are part of greatly contribute to people's personalities. Even the month of someone's birth makes a difference. A baby born around Christmas might feel his or her birthday always is overlooked. What if a child of a religious couple was born on Halloween? That might affect the way the parents treat the child, even if they do not mean for it to.

Those who lived through the Great Depression or know someone who has known the profound effect living through an economic crisis like that has on a person's approach to life. Once you have decided on an age for the characters, research some of the influential events during their generations and try to imagine how they affected your characters. Living through a major event like Pearl Harbor or 9/11 has an effect on a person even if he or she is not directly involved or affected by it. In those times of crisis, the nation bands together and everyone feels the losses as something personal. This can have a profound effect on a person's political views as they get older. It can cause them to think differently about a particular nation or race. In *Gran Torino*, Walt Kowalski, played by Clint Eastwood, is a Vietnam War veteran who feels his whole neighborhood is being taken over by immigrants. He wants nothing to do with the new neighbors, whom he knows little to nothing about. But after the neighbor family's son, Thao, attempts to steal his prized Gran Torino, he finds himself pulled into their world and slowly begins to enjoy the family. His transformation is so unlikely that it shocks his family when they learn of it after his death. Keep this in mind as you write. Just because a transformation is unlikely does not mean it is impossible. Just because you decide the view your character has at the start of the screenplay does not mean it is the view he or she has to keep as the screenplay progresses.

Who doesn't have a special love for the music and television shows of their childhood? Rather than having characters announce how old they are, referring to something they loved as a child can give the audience a clue to how old they are. A woman who says she loved Madonna as a teenager was probably going through those teen years in the '80s, the height of Madonna's popularity.

The way society has progressed over the last 20 or 30 years is also something to consider as you write. The American family structure is not the picture of two parents, two kids, a dog, and a picket fence anymore. Many adults, after attending college and beginning a career, are waiting longer to marry and have children. On the other hand, teenage pregnancy has become more acceptable in society and no longer bears the stigma it did in the '60s and '70s. Depending on the choices your characters make, they might be parents at a young age or only when they are much older. This also changes the dynamic they have within the family. A grandma who is in her 40s does different activities with the kids than a grandma in her 60s.

Name

Your characters might come into your mind already possessing their names. Other writers can spend hours trying to choose the perfect name for everyone in the movie. There are many possible ways to choose names for the characters in your screenplay. You can Google lists of the most popular names every year for boys and girls. Choosing a popular name can help the audience identify with the protagonist and characters. The children's names can be an indication of ethnic background or socioeconomic status. Keep in mind that popular names can vary from country to country or even within different regions of the country.

What's in a Name?

The name chosen for a child has more to do with the child's parents than the child his or herself. The bestselling book *Freakonomics* broke down what exactly a child's name says about the child's parents. In doing research, authors Dubner and Levitt determined that certain names are popular among a higher socioeconomic status and will then become popular among a lower income group about five years later. Once the name becomes popular in that lower income group, it will take a long time for it to become popular with the richer people again. They also found that giving your child a unique or made-up name can limit his or her job opportunities. Choosing a trendy name can suggest the parents are hip and young or that they are not concerned with individuality.

Incorporating Your Characters' Pasts

The biggest indicator of the future behavior of your character is his or her past. Let your audience know about the story behind your characters without boring them with backstory. One way to do this is to let the information come out naturally, as the pace of the movie dictates. Do not rush to let the audience in on the secrets, in the same way you would not make a new friend and begin instantly telling them about the hardships of your past. In a movie, the incidents that happen lead the truths to come out.

In *Thelma & Louise*, the best friends head out of town for the weekend. Thelma meets Harlan in a roadside bar, and he tries to rape her. Louise shoots him, not in the heat of the moment that she catches them, but right after, as he makes a comment. Scared of what will happen to them, Louise convinces Thelma they cannot go to the police. As they begin to run, Louise is the one to take charge and insists they go to Mexico but without passing through Texas. Before the film ends, the audience finds out that Louise was raped in Texas in her past, but the perpetrators were never punished.

Exposing this part of Louise's past shows us her motivation for much of what she does. If it was not for this experience, would Louise shoot Harlan, or would she allow him to walk away? Would they have gone directly to the police and offered the truth? Would they have made it to Mexico if they could have passed through Texas? Any of these decisions are responsible for the girls' ultimate demise. They all result from the one event in Louise's past.

Louise could have easily said to Thelma at the moment the incident happened with Harlan, "Hey Thelma, I was raped before in Texas; that's why I don't want to go to the police or pass through

Texas. Okay by you?" Certainly, Thelma and Louise seem to be good friends, and it is plausible that she would tell her friend about her past. But the movie is more suspenseful if Louise keeps her secret; it is more in keeping with her character and more truthful to the experience of a woman with a trauma in her past.

Get as specific as you can. Knowing the little details about your character and weaving them into the story make the characters more authentic. If your character is from the Midwest, do not leave it at just that. Think about where specifically. A farm in Iowa is a much different experience than growing up in a Cedar Rapids apartment building.

The Look of your Characters

Describing how your characters look is a tricky balance you must strike. You do not want to describe the character in too great of detail. This might bore the reader, and it cuts down on the casting possibilities. For example, this description might be too much:

> Candy Adams is a medium height woman, originally from Atlanta, with long blond hair and blue eyes. She is thin and sexy, and she currently is wearing a red Donna Karan suit and matching Manolo Blahniks. Her bright smile lights up every party in town.

Try to get to the heart of what is important about the character. The things that matter most in this example are Candy's southern roots and her social status. It might not matter whether she is blond or brunette. A better description might be:

> Candy Adams, 25, is a stylish, southern woman who loves God every bit as much as she does a good time.

By keeping the details about her appearance less specific, you allow the director more room to put his or her vision forward. Maybe they see Candy as a stylish Atlanta socialite who would never wear a cowboy hat unless she attends a rodeo. Or perhaps they want to cast a black or Latina actor as Candy.

Think about what is important to the plot. If your character has to be small enough to fit in a tunnel to escape from prison, you might want to mention he or she is short and skinny. Otherwise, leave the looks to the casting director.

Keeping track of your characters' pasts

It is hard to know how much preparation is too much. You do need to know a good deal about your characters before you start writing. Perhaps the worst thing about not planning before you begin writing is the interruption it causes in your writing process. Having to interrupt yourself and stopping to think take you out of that productive space and back into the planning stages. This can lead you to have an unproductive day or writer's block. Even if you did not plan all the characters' histories and traits before you started, you might want to keep a planning document as you decide things about your characters.

Do not forget, this is also where you create the reasons behind the character's actions. If you have decided your character has some kind of tic, you will have to plant the seeds for that in his or her background somewhere. If your character is a heartless womanizer, giving him a reason why he is afraid of love and commitment can save him from being a stereotype.

Then again, sometimes having everything outlined takes all the fun out of the creative process. Doing extensive amounts of research can help you procrastinate the actual writing part, which is the most important step and is sure to take the longest. At a certain point, you have to set research aside. As you come across facts or details you are unsure of, you can make a note and research them before your next writing session.

Once you decide something about your characters, it is good to keep track of it. You can create note cards with a background for each character, similar to the story cards that will be discussed in Chapter 6. If you prefer to keep notes on your computer, you can create a simple word document with the information. Those who have more knowledge about programming can create their own wikis with backgrounds and characters. If you use a screenwriting program like Final Draft®, you can add script notes to keep track of these ideas as you write. This way you can come back to it and consult on the details of your characters background. In life, sometimes it is hard to remember everything that has happened to you, never mind events you made up about someone else.

The Arc

People often complain a movie is boring because not enough happens to hold their interest. One of the likely reasons for this is the lack of character arc. In addition to going on a journey to get what he or she wants, your character should be going on an internal journey, a transformation. The Grinch in *Dr. Seuss' How The Grinch Stole Christmas* goes on a journey to Whoville, to steal all the trappings of Christmas from the Whos. But he ends up changing on the inside, and his heart grows two sizes that day. Though your protagonist's arc is the most prominent in the movie, all your characters should change over the course of the movie.

In *Jerry Maguire*, Jerry starts out as a typical sports agent, fast-talking and slick. Within the first few pages, he has a breakdown and writes his mission statement about the way sports management should be. It seems that Jerry has arced already. Movie over, right? Not quite. Jerry knows he wants to be better, but now he actually has to go out and make himself better. He quits his job, starts his new agency, works on Rod's career, and marries Dorothy. Movie over, right? Not quite. Jerry's marriage with Dorothy is still unresolved. It is not until we see Jerry running to get home to tell her that she completes him that we know he has truly changed.

Though Jerry's journey is the most important, Jerry's client, Rod Tidwell, also changes over the course of the movie. Rod goes from being a selfish whiner to being more of a team player. This makes him more successful and helps move Jerry's journey along, as well.

Writing to Help Understand Your Characters

A good way to cure writer's block can be to write something outside your outline, let your brain wander free for a little bit, and see where your creativity takes you. There can be advantages to writing extra scenes that are not intended for your final draft but that help explain the backstory or shed light on the story in other ways. This can be a fun way to practice in your characters' voices or get a better grasp of the dynamic between the two characters. Scenes you do not use can be used later as a sample of your work, in marketing and attracting attention to the screenplay, or online as part of a blog about the screenplay. You also can rework parts you like into another screenplay you write later on, maybe a sequel to your current feature.

If you do not want to write backstory or just want to cut loose creatively to help yourself get to know your characters, you can look for writing prompts online. A writing prompt usually gives you a location and situation to get you started on a scene. Some writing prompts to get started with:

- Your protagonist and your romance character go fishing and run across a bear.

- One of your characters out Black Friday shopping realizes the person he is beating with a frozen pizza to get to a cheap TV is someone he knows.

- Two of your characters are helping your protagonist move to a new house.

- One of your characters is giving birth to a baby.

- It is Halloween night and as many of your characters as you can work in are at the same party.

- One of your characters is taking a French cooking class.

- Two of your characters are at the running of the bulls.

- Your antagonist comes home to find a mysterious package at her door.

- Two of your characters are trapped in an elevator.

- Your antagonist is helping a woman who is having a baby.

- Your romance character is trying to get cast on a reality show.

- Your protagonist and your reflection are eating lunch at McDonald's®.

- Your antagonist is at a bank that is being robbed.

- Your romance character gets a haircut, and he hates it.

- Your protagonist is at the top of the Empire State Building.

- Your protagonist and your romance character are camping out in line for tickets to a concert.

- Your antagonist is on the first day at the new job.

- Your reflection is getting fired from a job.

Make Your Secondary Characters Memorable

Your secondary characters easily can become throwaways. We have all seen a movie in which we cannot remember most of the friends, only the main character. Here are some ways to combat this:

- Minimize the amount of secondary characters. Instead of a group of girlfriends, focus on one or two. In real life, a grown woman might have a group of girlfriends, but between jobs, family, and other scheduling conflicts, chances are they do not meet in a big group that often. Pairs or groups of three are more likely to meet. More likely still is that a character is close to a sibling or family member. Introducing a family member can be fun for a writer because it introduces different dynamics and can inspire all kinds of new subplots.

- Make each character's voice distinct. What is the point of having three unless they each add something to the story? Is your character a princess with a court of maidens waiting on her? Is she an insecure Hollywood starlet who needs to have her entourage around her constantly? Unless each character is adding something, think about cutting him or her and giving the lines to an existing character.

- Try to give your secondary characters (not the reflection or romance character; the extras that fill out the cast) equal amounts of screen time.

- Make sure each character is arcing. As your protagonist goes on a journey, the other characters go on a journey, too. Their journeys have to be less complicated, as they will get less screen time.

Structuring
Your Work

oing to the movies is like riding Space Mountain, the Disney® roller coaster that takes place entirely in the dark. As you wait to get on the ride, you hear the squeals and shouts of the people riding the ride. You know there will be loops and steep drops, but you do not know how the overall experience will be until you ride it. That is what going to a movie is like. You have seen the previews or heard reviews from friends, but you do not know exactly where the story is going to go, nor should you want to. The reason you go to the movie is the same as the reason you get on the roller coaster: You want to have fun and enjoy yourself. You want to be a little surprised but not too much.

For you as the writer, it also can be like riding the roller coaster in the dark. With the idea ripe in your mind and a blank document in front of you, it can be hard to know where the story begins unless you know where you are going and the stops you want to hit on the way. Outlining and structuring your screenplay is important, as it will help you to get the points you want to convey across to the viewer.

Structuring a screenplay is different from structuring any other work, such as a novel or stage play. A screenwriter has to provide a context, location, and story but has to allow the work to be open to interpretation by the director and actors. *More information on how much direction to include in your screenplay is available in Chapter 10.* But like any other story, a movie script has a beginning, middle, and end. The beginning of your movie has to get the viewer's interest, the middle has to hold the viewer's interest, and the end has to give a satisfying resolution to the story and wrap up the subplots.

The Three-Act Structure

If you hope to structure a film suitable for sale in Hollywood, the first step is to master the three-act structure. Since being suggested by Syd Field, the screenwriting guru, the three-act structure has become the Hollywood standard. Just about every movie you have ever seen is structured in this way, and once you learn about it, you will notice it every time you watch a movie. In the three-act structure, the whole of your movie is split into three acts, with a major plot point that serves as the turning point between each.

The beginning of your screenplay is Act One, the middle is Act Two, and the end is Act Three. Act One introduces the viewer to the movie. Act Two is where the most action happens. Act Three brings the movie to a satisfying close. Remember that one page of screenplay equals one minute of screen time. Most movies are about two hours long; so most screenwriters aim for 120 pages of screenplay. This is just a goal and can vary in the finished product. The story of your movie might only take 100 pages to tell, which is also fine. For a first-time screenwriter hoping to get noticed, it is vital not to go over this page count. If nothing else, it shows the studio you are able to edit your own work.

Act One: The Setup

This act should run from the beginning of the screenplay to page 30. The audience has paid their money, grabbed their popcorn and drink, and watched what seemed like an endless number of previews, all to go on a journey to a location they do not know. Act One is where they get to see who and what the movie is about. This is when you let them see the location of the movie, the people the movie is about, the world they live in, and most important, what it is the main character wants — the reason for the movie.

In *Bad Teacher*, we are introduced to Elizabeth Halsey, a self-centered, irresponsible teacher played by Cameron Diaz. As the film opens, the faculty and staff at John Adams Middle School are bidding her goodbye as she resigns to begin her married life. She stomps out to her Mercedes Benz and reverses in high speed away from the school, oblivious to the children standing nearby and the school bus she cuts off. She hurls a final insult at the school as the peels away. Though Elizabeth goes on to top herself, showing us again and again why she is such a bad teacher, this opener quickly introduces us to her character: self-centered and superficial, more concerned with labels and money than people and their feelings.

Getting the viewer's attention

The first images of a film are the ones to grab the viewer's attention. Think of the scene you would like to set for them. Is your movie a lighthearted, summer love story or a tersely paced thriller? How can you get the viewer to be interested from the start? Begin with an image that draws their interest. Pull them in with what they see. Start right in the middle of the action.

Think of our film example from a couple chapters ago, *Getting Out of Grossville*, which seems to be shaping up to be a romantic comedy. The opening can convey some of these facts for us: shots of the grocery store setting, a generic suburban town, maybe a sign that shows the town's population. Maybe we see teens lurking around a convenience store or a fast-food joint, looking for trouble to get into. When the film opens, Emma does not take her job seriously. To establish this for the viewer, maybe the first real scene of the movie takes place as Emma and Elaine hide in the meat freezer at the grocery store, eating a birthday cake they have stolen from the bakery department. This scene shows us the location where a good deal of the movie takes place and gives us an easy way to relate back to what most of the movie will be about: Emma's quest for a better job and a better life.

If you have a more involved story, or a more complicated concept, consider how you can communicate it with images. This is often done well in children's movies when the viewer is too impatient to sit through a long explanation. *Alvin and the Chipmunks* opens with the chipmunks harmonizing as they pack nuts into a tree. Thus, they speak, they sing, but in other ways, they behave like regular chipmunks. The entire premise is set up from this opening before a word of dialogue is spoken.

The first ten pages

No reader will read past the tenth page of your screenplay unless compelled to do so. You have these ten pages to show them everything they want to know. Try to address the following questions:

- Who are the people in your story? The main characters and even your important secondary characters should come into the film early unless the plot dictates otherwise. They have a lot to accomplish, and they need time to do it. Also, the earlier you put them in, the less the audience is likely to feel they were rushed just to make the ending work.

- Where do they live, work, and play? Give the audience an idea of who your characters are in their day-to-day lives. What are their daily routines? How will these routines change as the story progresses?

- What does your protagonist want? What journey is he or she about to go on? Why he or she chooses to accept the challenge or chase the desire is for you to explain.

- What is he or she up against? Who is the antagonist and why is he or she standing in the protagonist's way?

- What kind of movie is this? Set the tone for the movie. Is this a laugh-a-minute comedy or a drama that requires careful attention?

Remember, you do not have to reveal everything. Give the audience a glimpse of each of these aspects of the screenplay. Make sure there is still some suspense, something to compel them to keep watching. Keep the locations of your scenes creative and as visually interesting as you can. *Some advice for keeping scenes visually interesting will be given in Chapter 6.*

The first ten pages of the screenplay are also the best place to plant the setups that will pay off later in the screenplay. If your character will save himself or herself from the bad guys in the third act using championship kung fu skills, make sure the kung fu comes up within the first ten pages. Make sure you keep track of all of the setups and pay each one off, as the story will feel unfinished to the viewer if some of the setups are not resolved.

In the beginning of *Mean Girls*, we are introduced to Cady Heron and her family. Cady explains that she has spent her life in Africa, where her parents were conducting field research. Cady has never been to a real high school before, and her parents are somewhat out of touch with the day-to-day life of teenagers. This pays off several times in the movie. Right away, we see Cady's parents seeing her off to school with the type of advice better suited to a child on the first day of kindergarten. On Halloween, Cady is shocked by the sexy costumes the other girls wear. And several times, Cady compares the rituals and interactions of high school to those of the animals she interacted with in Africa. As you plant setups in your screenplay, try to think of multiple ways they can pay off.

Setting up the motivations of your characters is always important. For the audience to make the leap with your character, you have to explain the reason they are leaping. If the audience cannot buy the premise, they will not get involved in the hero's journey.

In *Yes Man*, Jim Carrey plays loan officer Carl Allen. Within the first ten pages of the screenplay, the audience sees that Carl is doing all right at work but has shut down his personal life. Since getting divorced, he ignores his friends and obligations; he chooses instead to stay home alone and watch movies. When he misses a friend's engagement party, the friend warns him that he will end up all alone if he does not change, and he takes the warning seriously. He ends up going to the seminar where he will pledge to say yes to every new opportunity, changing his life permanently. The glimpse we get of his life in the first ten pages helps us understand Carl's state of mind and the kind of person he is.

Remember that film is a visual medium. Any chance you have to use a picture to show your audience the idea you are trying to convey is one you should take. *Sleeping with the Enemy* could have opened with Laura Burney, played by Julia Roberts, confessing to a friend or family member over coffee that her controlling husband is abusing her. This might be a touching moment if scripted well, but it would not be interesting visually. Instead, we see her making sure towels are hung evenly and turning the cans in her cupboard so the labels face the front uniformly. We see her husband, Martin, being loving, the handsome couple they make, the American dream, Cape Cod style. This setup is what makes the chill run down the viewer's spine when Martin loses it and beats Laura for the first time. It reminds us of the shame and secrets that hide victims of domestic violence every day.

The event

Some call it the incident, others call it the catalyst, still others the inciting event — the thing that happens to set your protagonist on his or her journey; it spurs him or her into action. Maybe it is learning a new piece of information that changes his or her life, or maybe it is a call to action. Something in life needs fixing and can wait no longer. Perhaps it is news of some form. It could be a death. Whatever it is, it has to be dealt with immediately, and the protagonist has no time to lose. This event takes place around page ten of the story before any of the plot points. It is the first thing in the movie that causes the protagonist to get moving on the path he or she will take. In American Beauty, Lester learns he may be losing his job, which causes him to start re-evaluating his life. This event sets the story in motion.

For our story, *Getting Out of Grossville*, Emma seeing the posting for the manager position might be the event. That is a reasonable story: A girl wants a better life, sees a job posting, and goes for a promotion. Except it is not interesting. Let's consult Emma's motivation. Maybe Emma is a bridesmaid in a friend's wedding. At the wedding shower, which she tries hard to make chic and fun, she overhears her friends gossiping about how her taste is tacky and her shower a flop, that she will never be more than a small town grocery cashier. She goes home and tells Mom all about it, but Mom is a little condescending. Mom suggests that Emma get comfortable with where she is in life or consider asking her friend for tips on marrying up. Now when Emma sees the job posting, it means more to her than just a better job. It means redemption. The audience can relate to this journey.

Plot point one

At the end of page 30 comes your first plot point, another incident that changes the action. It pushes the story forward, but in a different direction. It raises the stakes. Whatever plot point one is, it is usually a surprise to the protagonist. In this way, it is similar to the incident that set the protagonist in motion on their journey. But the first plot point should be a bigger event, something that affects the protagonist even more.

If we are back on the roller coaster in the dark, the first ten pages of the script is where the track just in front of us is illuminated. We can see where we are going, but not for long. The plot point is the unexpected drop in the roller coaster's track, the curve we do not see coming. Our hero or heroine is happily pottering along in his or her quest that started with the event, and plot point one comes along to make his or her journey a little more complicated, a little harder to get.

A plot point can also be stunning, as in *American Beauty*. Plot point one occurs when Lester Burnham, played by Kevin Spacey as a suburban loser having a midlife crisis, gets dragged to see his daughter cheerlead. As he watches his daughter's friend Angela dance, rose petals erupt from her, signifying Lester's latent desires that are now coming to the surface. As Angela continues, the rest of the room falls away and Lester becomes lost in what is now an intimate fantasy.

Back to *Getting Out of Grossville*. The event was Emma seeing the job posting. Now, throughout Act One, we see Emma doing well at her job, impressing her bosses, and making friends with the customers. Emma develops a crush on one of her regulars, a guy whom she slips extra steaks into the paper for because she knows he has not been able to find regular work since graduating from college. In plot point one, she finds out that he has applied for a job where she works, which she is initially excited about. Until she finds out he is ultimately after the manager job she hopes to get, and because of his fancy college degree and retail experience, he is now her fiercest competition. The action in Acts Two and Three will move in a different direction than in Act One. Now Emma has to balance trying to look good at her job with making him look bad, all without him noticing. This plot point has changed her life more than the first incident did.

Act Two: The Confrontation

This act should run from page 30 to page 70. This is the part of the story where life becomes difficult for your protagonist. Whatever it is that the protagonist wants, this is where he or she proves how passionate he or she is about it. If your protagonist is hoping to succeed in a sport, this would be the part of the movie where we see practicing, running up flights of stairs, waking up early to run laps, and putting in all the hard work it will take to win.

This also can be the fun part of your screenplay. The characters get to play with whatever toys you have given them in the first act. If they robbed a bank and got away with a suitcase full of cash, this is where they get to spend the money on all their wild desires. If you have a crazy image you want to see created in your movie, this is a good place for it.

You also have time here to develop your subplots and let your characters come out. If your characters are going to fall in love, this is where they will take the time to do it.

If there are things you need to set up for the third act, this is where to do it. If you want to have your protagonist run away to Brazil at the end of the crime caper, make sure you plant the fact that he or she always has wanted to go to Carnival somewhere in the second act.

The Visual Medium

Film is a visual medium. Think about what will be exciting and fun on the screen, the moments that people will remember and discuss with their coworkers later on. Imagine things that are unexpected and shocking. Think about the following images from films:

- In *The Money Pit*, the main staircase in the mansion collapses out from under Tom Hanks.

- The White House was destroyed by aliens in *Independence Day*.

- The whale jumps over the boy and into the open water in *Free Willy*.

- A cruise ship crashes into an island town and destroys it in *Speed 2: Cruise Control*.

The second act can be notoriously hard to keep interesting for an audience. One way to combat this is to make things difficult for your protagonist. The problems in your protagonist's life should get worse as Act Two progresses and builds the action toward plot point two. The worse things get for your hero, the better for your audience. No one wants to watch a movie in which nothing happens. Throw everything you can at him or her.

In *Getting Out of Grossville*, how can we complicate the second act for Emma? The first way is to remove her most obvious ally, Elaine. Perhaps Elaine gets fired. Or maybe it is more interesting if Elaine stays on but now has a new supervisor who watches Elaine like a hawk. Maybe there is a problem customer who continues to come in and give Emma a hard time.

As the second act goes on, the problems should snowball, getting worse and worse, up until plot point two. The more difficulties and obstacles the protagonist has to overcome, the more interesting the viewer will find the second act. If the protagonist gets his or her desire too easily, the audience will feel it was not a journey worth going on.

Plot point two

At plot point two, the stakes are raised again; the action is again pushed in another direction. This time, our protagonist is either dropped to a new low of lows or raised to a high, possibly a false one. If your film has a time element, plot point two is a good time to remind the audience of this upcoming deadline and the pressure it brings on your characters. A classic example is a story in which a character has realized he or she is in love with another character that is on his or her way to the airport to leave forever. This makes the time element obvious and catapults the audience into the run to the airport with the main character.

For an example of a second plot point, let's go back to the movie *American Beauty*, There is some room for interpretation, but most agree that the second plot point happens when Lester is unable to sleep with Angela.

Problems in the second act

The second act of a movie is notoriously the hardest to write. Sustaining the story and the suspense through the middle of the movie can be difficult. The pace of your movie can be hard to maintain because it is so long compared to the other two acts. Changing the tone or story of the movie too much can confuse your audience and cause them to feel dissatisfied, as though neither of the stories is sufficiently resolved.

In 2008's *Hancock*, Will Smith plays an alcoholic superhero that goes only by the name Hancock. As the movie begins, Hancock saves an executive named Ray, played by Jason Bateman, from being crushed by a train. Ray begins to see that Hancock is misunderstood and tries to help him rehab his image. Ray's wife, Mary, still feels like the majority of the city and distrusts Hancock. In the second act, the story changes dramatically; Mary reveals to Hancock that she is also a superhero and is his mate. The movie goes from a dark comedy about a gruff superhero with problems to a romance story about star-crossed lovers reuniting after 80 years. The film confused some viewers, who felt it was too much like watching two different movies.

To keep the tone and action of the movie steady, make sure the mission your protagonist is on is a constant presence. Even if you veer off into subplots, make sure that in every few scenes, you are addressing the main story line.

Act Three: The Resolution

Wrapping up the story of your screenplay can be difficult. The protagonist is at a turning point in his or her life, or at least the portion of it your script tells. Protagonists often are taking one last shot at the things they want so much. Sometimes they are doing so armed with new information or new skills they believe will make them successful. Or, the protagonist has no choice but to confront the issue even if he or she is not prepared because someone else has confronted him or her with it. This act should run from page 70 to page 100. Within this act should be the climax of the film, a few pages from the end. The last few pages of the screenplay are for you to wrap up any loose ends and leave the audience satisfied that the story was resolved.

Schadenfreude

Why is it we so enjoy watching the miseries of other people on the screen? The psychological term is schadenfreude, a German word that refers to the pleasure one derives from seeing another person's misfortune. In English, the closest word would perhaps be to gloat. As there is no real equivalent word in English, the German word is used in English as well as in some other languages. The exact reasons why we get pleasure from watching other people suffer are still up for debate. Some research suggests people feel better about themselves after seeing the misfortunes of others. In movies, audiences particularly enjoy seeing someone get what he or she deserves. But if you pile the drama on too thick, viewers will give your movie the dreaded assessment of being too much like a soap opera. Things should come to a conclusion, but a reasonable one. Let your characters and story dictate how the story should end and what needs to be said.

Three-Act Structure Case Study: *Runaway Bride*

The three-act structure is easiest to understand with an example. Written by the Ephron sisters, a respected writing team, *Runaway Bride* is a big budget romantic comedy that makes a good example because the plot points are easy to identify.

Opening image

The movie begins with exactly what the audience came to see: a bride on horseback, riding like there is no way she wants to be caught. We know, for obvious reasons, that this is our main character, doing what she does best. There is no need to establish any further who she is. A lesser screenwriter might have a crowd chasing after her or the groom yelling "Maggie!" But in this case, the screenwriters trust that this glimpse of our beautiful heroine will suffice to pique our interest. From here, the script teases the viewer a little bit by cutting away to introduce the other major character, Ike. This is a setup, already, to a payoff later in the movie. As we watch Ike go about his daily business, we hear him on the phone pitching stories to an answering machine. This allows us to learn many things about Ike's character: He is a journalist with a weekly column. He is feeling uninspired, and like most writers, needs some validation and encouragement so he can get moving on the column. But because his friend does not answer, he seeks the validation in a local bar.

The incident

Ike meets a guy in a bar who tells him about Maggie. We have already seen that Ike is desperate, entrenched in writer's block, hoping for something to write about. So, it is understandable that he would take this information and run with it without doing research. Many members of the public have the belief that journalists rush to print without checking facts as a common practice anyway, so it is not a stretch of the imagination.

Plot point one

Next, Maggie reacts to Ike's column and sends the editor a scathing letter that points out the 15 errors in his story. Ike is summarily fired. This firing is the first plot point: It is unexpected for Ike, and it causes him to jump to action in a way that the audience has not foreseen. Yet, this is believable because Ike works at a large national paper that cannot have stories with numerous factual errors running without taking action. Offered the chance to redeem himself and an opportunity to see his byline in *GQ*, Ike decides to track Maggie down and sniff out the real story.

The second act

As Ike researches about Maggie, we learn more about both of them. We get to see Maggie's past weddings on tape, and each has its own comic twist. The first time, she drags the ring bearer out with her as she passes the altar and just keeps walking out the back door. The second time, she has a hippie wedding in which she crowd surfs to the altar and runs away by jumping on a passing dirt bike. The third time is the time we saw at the start of the film when she has run away on horseback. This is the payoff from the setup at the opening of the movie. The real discovery of this last wedding is the groom, who turns out to be Ike's source for the newspaper article, the mysterious man from the bar. The second act hijinks are there as Maggie and Ike meet in person for the first time, and Maggie and her friend Peggy dye Ike's hair various colors while they feed him bad information. Instead of a traditional wedding shower, Maggie has a luau in a barn. We find out one of Maggie's almost grooms is now a priest. Grandma offers her opinion on Ike's butt. We also find out that Maggie is engaged again, with the wedding date approaching. This adds a time element to the story. The audience knows that the climax of the story likely will be at this wedding. Ike points out to Maggie what no one in her life is saying, that she is so confused about who she really is she doesn't even know how she likes her eggs because she always orders the same breakfast as her fiancé.

At the midpoint of the movie, the rehearsal of Maggie's wedding to Bob, Maggie and Ike realize they are in love. Immediately, Maggie and Bob break up and Maggie and Ike fall into a new romance. As they realize how they feel about each other, we see shots of them spending time together, playing cards, and falling in love. Because the wedding already is booked and the date is already saved, they decide to get married. Ike is confident he knows the real Maggie, the one none of the other guys bothered to get to know. He is sure Maggie will make it to the altar for their wedding.

Plot point two

In the second plot point, Maggie tries to make it down the altar the fifth and final time to meet Ike. In an ironic moment, Maggie worries the media circus outside the church will cause Ike to change his mind and become a runaway groom. Reporters clamor for shots of the once cynical and dismissive Ike, showing up at the church in his tuxedo ready to pledge his life to Maggie. Vendors sell T-shirts with Maggie's face on them. Ike's friends show up; his half of the church is full of black suits and cell phones. The other half is filled with the residents of Hale, some hoping against hope that Maggie will make it this time, others with money on bets that she will not. As Maggie tries to make it down the aisle, we are on the edge of our seats, waiting to see if she will make it. She keeps eye contact with Ike as she walks steadily toward him, and it seems that this time will be the one that counts. But then, as a guest takes a picture, the flash forces Ike to close his eyes. Maggie turns and runs. Though Ike chases her through the church, across a children's classroom and out a window, she jumps on a

FedEx® truck and lets it take her away. Ike runs behind the truck screaming her name, and the reporters get an eyeful of their former colleague thoroughly humiliating himself.

At the end of the second act, it seems that all is lost. Despite all Maggie's assurances that this is for real, the time that she will make it to the altar, she has run away again, and Ike has become a national laughingstock. His face is on the front of his former paper. They are obviously going to break up and never be able to put the relationship back together. How can they possibly make this better?

The third act

We see Maggie finally taking charge of her life. She confronts her father about his teasing and starts selling the lamps she designs. We see her trying every kind of eggs to determine how she likes them. This is a symbolic scene: Maggie is making a commitment to finding out who she is and what she likes. When we see her return to Ike, we know that she has changed.

The climax

Ike finds Maggie in his apartment waiting to tell him about the changes she has made, the things she has done to change for the better. She tells him how she likes her eggs, turns in her running shoes, and pops the question.

The conclusion

Ike and Maggie finally get married, a small wedding with only their closest friends invited. We see the townspeople hearing the good news and celebrating. Ike and Maggie have one last kiss, and they fade to black.

Subplots

There are many subplots in *Runaway Bride*. Most of them involve Maggie's friends and family and her relationships with them.

- Maggie's father, her relationship with him, and his alcoholism. This subplot begins in Act Two, when Ike sees Maggie pick up her dad from the bar because he is too drunk to drive. It resolves itself in Act Three, when Maggie confronts her dad and says he might not like having a daughter with problems, but she does not like having a drunk for a father. Her grandmother backs her up, and the point seems to hit home with him. Although the audience knows Dad's alcoholism is far from resolved, we feel that the family is finally ready to deal with it.

- Maggie's relationship with her best friend Peggy. Peggy is the cheerful and eternally supportive best friend, played by Joan Cusack. Maggie comes to realize, by seeing their relationship through Ike's eyes, that she has not always been the best of friends to Peggy.

- Ike's relationship with his ex-wife and her new husband. Unlike most people, Ike is involved in the marriage of his ex-wife and his friend. As the movie plays on, we see that their lives are tightly interwoven.

- Maggie as the town laughingstock. Though Ike originally contributes to this problem, he eventually feels bad about the way Maggie is treated at the town bridal shop and during her luau, where the guests roast Maggie about her past. Though it is all done in good humor and Maggie keeps a smiling face, Ike sees how much it really hurts her. This story line is somewhat resolved in the last few minutes of the movie, as we see the town celebrating Maggie and Ike's good news.

A screenplay can have multiple subplots as long as they are all developed well and do not detract from the main story. As you devote time to these subplots throughout the movie, do not forget to check back in with the main story line. Wherever possible, combine scenes to accomplish both purposes and advance both story lines. The scene where Ike accompanies Maggie to the bridal salon advances the main story line of Maggie attempting to get married to Bob, the main story line of Maggie and Ike falling in love, and the subplot about Maggie's reputation in town for being a flake. It also gives Ike a chance to be chivalrous and ingratiate himself with the audience.

Alternate Ways to Approach Structure

In the book *Screenwriting for Hollywood*, well-respected screenwriting guide, Michael Hauge offers the idea of measuring plot points and acts in terms of percentage of screenplay. As Hauge points out, not all screenplays have the same page count; so counting the pages does not work in every instance. Instead, Hauge suggests measuring events in terms of where they fall by percentages. According to Hauge's numbers, the event should go 10 percent of the way into the script. So, if your script is 100 pages, it should fall on page ten.

Films that do not adhere to the three-act structure

There have been successful movies that seem, on first watch, not to adhere to the three-act structure. The example given most often for this is the movie *Memento,* a cult classic released in 2000. Christopher Nolan, now famous as the director of *Inception,* crafted *Memento.* The movie tells the story of a man with retrograde amnesia. Every day he wakes up a blank slate. He became this way after his wife's murder and is trying to investigate and avenge her death. To do this in his condition, he has adapted some techniques, including tattooing himself all over with words and numbers important to his investigation and taking Polaroids of people, which he marks to show whether they are his allies or enemies. The movie is told half in chronological order, and the other half backward, which gives the viewer a taste of what it is like to have his condition. Although there are still plot points in this movie, the way they are presented makes the viewer pay close attention to the film to recognize them.

Another movie that seems to defy convention is the German movie *Run Lola Run.* The script of the movie is actually a traditionally structured story but with three different endings, shown one after the other. Each time the story ends, we return to the same point in the story. The movie begins with Lola, who gets a call from her boyfriend Manni. Manni needs Lola to get $100,000, the money that he owes a drug dealer but accidentally left on a subway car. Manni needs the money within the next 20 minutes, and the only thing he can think of is to rob a grocery store. Lola decides to ask her father, the bank manager, for the money and tells Manni not to do anything, that she will be there. She hangs up the phone and runs down the stairs. It is at this point that the three different movies of the film start. The second and third acts of the three versions of the story are all different. The first time, Lola runs to her father's bank to ask him for the money. He refuses and tells her he is tired of his marriage, tired of her mother, and tired of her because she is not even really his child. Lola joins Manni in robbing the store, and in the aftermath, she is shot by a police officer. The film now returns to the point where Lola hangs up the phone and runs down the stairs. The second time, a dog trips her on her staircase. She stumbles on her father talking to his mistress, and in a rage, she robs the bank. She gets away with the money but this time Manni is killed, run over as he crosses a street to meet her. The final time, Lola runs faster than ever. Manni finds the homeless guy who picked up the bag of money he forgot and trades the man his gun for the bag of money. In this last and final reality, Lola and Manni both live and walk away with money Lola won. The story does follow a three-act structure but each act is shorter, to allow the time to show the multiple paths Lola might take. To accommodate this, rather than have subplots, the lives of the people that Lola intersects with are shown in Polaroid® pictures that flash on the screen. The Polaroids show the supporting character's future unfolding. A stranger who bumps into Lola is shown having a child, losing the child, and then kidnapping another one.

Outlining
Your Work

*N*ow you have had the idea for your screenplay marinating in your brain for a while. You have thought it over: each character, their journeys, things you want to see happen, and the places you want to see them happen in. The idea for your screenplay might seem so large that it fills all the space in your brain. All of the details are in there somewhere, and as soon as you start on it, it will practically write itself. Until you do sit down to write it, and you find the idea is much smaller than you thought. All you come up with is a few words of dialogue, a handful of locations, and no way to get from points A to B. Or perhaps things have gone in the opposite direction, and the idea has become too big, too hard to wrangle.

Feeling like your screenplay idea is too much for you to map out entirely in your head is normal. A screenplay is a complicated story that involves many people and their journeys. You only get to show two hours worth of your hero's life, and if you do not properly detail how the hero gets to his or her conclusion, you risk leaving the audience unfulfilled. Where will you plant the setups, and how can you make sure each one is paid off? These are the things outlining the screenplay will help you keep track of.

A conventional outline, like you would create for a story or novel, is not practical for a screenplay. In even the simplest of screenplays, you have several people to keep up with. Trying to list everything that happens to each character in a long document is not really going to be as useful to you as it could be. You need a form of outline that can be easily tinkered with, that is portable, and that allows you to view a large amount of information in segments or together.

You can outline your screenplay in several different ways, but the accepted method involves some kind of card system: Each card gives a snapshot of a scene in the movie. You can measure a scene by starting it in a location and finishing it when your characters exit the location or you feel the action has completed itself. For your cards, each time your characters change location, begin a new card.

By looking at the index card for a scene, you will be able to tell where the scene takes place, the people involved, and the major action the scene accomplishes for the overall plot. Once you have all the scenes outlined on a card, you can start deciding how the cards fit together. By the time you start writing, each scene will be outlined and ready for you to write. This can help you break down the task of writing a screenplay, which seems immense at the start, into manageable segments. You can write one scene a day, two to three pages, and be done your first draft in a month and a half.

Some people call this process story carding; some call it the writer's board. It usually involves standard sized index cards, pinned or taped to a bulletin board or some other flat surface and divided into four rows. Put together, these cards make up the whole of your screenplay. The board allows you to see your screenplay in as easy and abbreviated a form as possible: the high and low points, the love story, and how the subplots are wound in. As you look at the board, you will be able to see where the action is intense and where it slows down, where the story really begins and where it ends. You can see how your subplots are woven into the main story and whether your secondary characters are getting enough screen time.

Making the Cards

At this point, you should have your logline, which gives you the who, what, why, and when of the story. You might not know exactly where the scenes you have in mind fit in the overall structure of the screenplay. Most likely, you do not have all of the scenes necessary to tell the whole story already in mind, but do not worry too much about that at this stage. The story card process is where you can indulge yourself and have some fun. This is the first step of your outlining process to help you see which scenes will bring the story together. All you need are the mental pictures of what you want to see in your finished script.

Breaking your scenes down into 40 to 60 index cards is daunting. It becomes a little more daunting when you consider that four of those cards will be reserved for titles, giving you even fewer cards to tell your story on. You might think it seems an unreasonably small number. Yet setting a goal of 40 to 60 puts a limit on how long the outlining process will last and keeps the board manageable. Once you start, you might find it hard to create that many cards, especially the ones needed to fill out the second act.

Think of your mind as a toy vending machine, the one with the mechanical claw you maneuver with a joystick that descends into the pile of toys. The scenes you have in your mind are the toys, and your job is to grab the best ones and get them out of your brain and into the screenplay. The scenes that have been in your brain forever, the ones that you can see perfectly when you close your eyes are the big teddy bears, the ones you obviously want. But if you look closer into the machine, underneath them you might see a real prize, an iPod® that will last much longer than the teddy bear. The scenes that take awhile to think about and unearth can turn out to be the best ones.

At this stage, do not limit yourself or be too critical of your ideas. But keep in mind some criteria so you do not waste time creating a bunch of scenes that will not get written. The scenes have to make the movie's main plot move forward. Even if they are fun and lighthearted, they need to contribute to the overall story line. They should have some action and a conflict between the characters.

Each story card should follow the same format. Across the top, write the information about the scene location. This also will be the heading on the page of script when you write the scene. List

INT (short for interior) or EXT (for exterior), then the location, for example, GRANDMA'S HOUSE, then whether the scene happens in the DAY or at NIGHT.

Next, write a synopsis of the most important part of the scene. What does the scene accomplish in the overall action of the film. Do not include extra details such as "The hero arrives, takes his jacket off, and sits down." Get directly to the most important points of the scene, such as his telling his wife he got laid off from work. If the scene is does not advance the plot or the major subplots, you might have to cut it or combine it with another. Keeping these cards as simple as possible is the best option, that way they can be switched in the overall order as you lay them out in the next step of the process.

The story card for a scene in *Getting Out Of Grossville* might read:

```
┌─────────────────────────────────────────────────┐
│ INT-DELI COUNTER-DAY                              │
│                                                   │
│   Emma finds out about manager position.          │
│                                                   │
│                                                   │
│                                                   │
│                                                   │
└─────────────────────────────────────────────────┘
```

This is one of the earlier scenes in the movie, before Emma has decided to change her ways. In this scene, Emma might have just arrived at work, hungover and reluctant to do any real work because it is Saturday. As she clocks in, she finds out two of her co-workers have called in sick, and she will be staffing the deli counter alone. She usually does not work that position and has no idea where anything is and no one to ask. She finds out about the manager position while eavesdropping on the manager and trying to help a customer at the same time. You already might have all of this in mind for the scene. But not all of this should appear on the index card. What matters to the overall story line is that Emma finds out about the new job posting. This bit of information will push the plot forward and advance Emma's journey to get what she wants. The rest are extras that make the scene interesting, but they are not the part driving the story forward.

Create a story card for each scene you know you will need to make the movie make sense. For example, say your movie is a crime caper. Without knowing anything about the plot, we know there will have to be a scene in which the actual crime is committed. There will be at least one scene when the crime is planned. To resolve the plot, there will need to be a scene where the perpetrator gets away or gets caught. As you create the cards for these basic moments, you might find a bit of a domino effect happening. More scenes are needed to make these scenes make sense. Why is your hero in this caper? Maybe you need a scene showing what motivated him to perpetrate this crime. How did he know the security guard would not be at his post at 10 p.m.? Give the audience a scene in which the hero does surveillance on the security guard to find out his routine. In a movie, it is not enough simply to tell the audience your hero prepared for a crime; it is better to show them.

Subplots

Your hero is off on an exciting journey that will change his or her life. As the people around him or her notice something big happening, they will want to participate, too. Your secondary characters are not content to be left in the dark while exciting things are happening to the hero, their friend, or relative. The stories that happen to your secondary characters will become your subplots. Subplots can affect or contribute to the main story line without the hero being in them directly. Sometimes your hero also will get involved in a subplot, usually a love story. Subplots might come about organically, as you write the story. Your character might wander into a situation you find too intriguing to let go of. They might have a friend who captures your imagination. These subplots add to the overall story. The secondary characters add pieces to the puzzle, painting a fuller image for you to consider. They present the same story, but from a different angle, and they offer the audience a slightly different take on events.

As you create a subplot, think about the following things:

- How are the events presented in this subplot different than the events presented in the main plot? The subplot should complement the main story line but not exactly echo it. In *My Big Fat Greek Wedding*, the main plot follows Toula, the daughter of strict Greek parents, as she starts to take charge and change her life. In a subplot, her brother is inspired by her success to take some classes himself and pursue his artistic talents. This makes Toula feel good, but it also shows the audience how far Toula has come, from the daughter seen as a failure to being an inspiration to her brother.

- How often does this subplot retell a situation presented in the main plot? Subplots should tie into what is happening to the main character, but they do not have to replay moments that have already been shown to the audience.

- How is the viewer/reader's experience heightened by this plotline? Some subplots put the audience in a superior position. This is where the audience knows things the characters do not. This creates a different kind of suspense for the audience. Say the subplot shows your audience the killer planning a murder. They know the killer is loose in the house while the characters enter. Now they are squirming in their seats while the family unpacks groceries and starts making dinner, not knowing the killer is hiding upstairs.

- Does your subplot have a distinct beginning, middle, and end of its own? The subplot needs to resolve itself just the same way that the main plot needs to conclude. The difference here is that the ending of the subplot does not need to be the end of the movie. As the subplots resolve themselves, they might contribute details that will be significant for the main plot.

Subplots on story cards

The subplots are important to the structure of the screenplay, and because they need to be tracked as well, they have to appear on some story cards. You can add an individual story card for the scenes of a subplot, or you can combine them with existing scenes. Let's say one of the subplots in the grocery store is Elaine, Emma's friend, and her budding romance with a new guy at the bakery. Each is too shy to approach the other. The scene where Emma finds out about the job posting just happens to be the same scene where Elaine, who comes to Emma's rescue at the deli counter, sees the guy for the first time. She stares at him as he wheels the bakery cart by. Our story card now reads:

INT-DELI COUNTER-DAY
Emma finds out about manager position.
Elaine sees the baker for the first time.

Marking the Cards

So now, you have your cards. This might make things clearer, but it also can increase your confusion because what you have written on the card is a simple recap of the scene's main action; it does not help you to keep track of the subplots, characters, or their progress. For this reason, many screenwriters will mark the cards in some way to show which subplots and characters are advanced in this scene. Some people will mark the cards with dots, check marks, or other symbols in various colors. For example, a card that advances a romance subplot can be marked with a heart or a red dot. The colors help you easily see how the subplots are featured throughout the screenplay. See a wealth of pink dots near the start of the movie but none after the midpoint? Maybe the subplot is being neglected, or maybe it simply resolves itself early on. Other writers like to mark the cards with letters or initials of the characters featured in the scene. Still others will mark the cards with the conflict and how it resolves itself, as well as the emotional change involved for your characters. For example, if you have a card in which Jim and Bob are in a fight, and Bob loses, which causes him great embarrassment in front of his wife, you might mark the card that Bob starts happy but ends up embarrassed. The card for that scene might look like this:

INT-ROADHOUSE SALOON-NIGHT
Bob and Jim fight in front of Brenda. Bob loses.
Bob: happy ↑ embarrassed ↓
Jim: angry ↓ triumphant ↑

Suddenly, the writing you have to undertake seems much easier.

You have a few more things to think about before you start the writing, but the index cards might be making ideas bubbles up in your brain. You might have ideas, a line or two of dialogue in mind that you really want to use in one scene, more about the location, or some detailed information you want to remember. You can add these details to the board in a few ways. Some writers add sticky notes to the card with the other ideas they have. The risk is that the note loses its stick and falls off the card. However, if you do not procrastinate and you get the writing done in a timely way, it should not present a problem. You also can write these details on the back of the index card. When the card is laid on a table or pinned to a board, these details will not be visible to distract you from the scene. Another way is to create an index system for the cards. Once you are sure you have the cards in their final order, you can assign each card a number, then make a corresponding document on your computer that shows all the extra information on that scene. For example:

Scene 46-Church Parking Lot.
Shauna wears a pastel pink suit and a large white hat with a pink ribbon. Shauna's car is a Hyundai Elantra. Todd comes over to recruit her for the bake sale. Todd says "sweet treats" too many times.

Finding the Conflict

Turn on your television at 10 a.m. any weekday, and you will see a selection of trash television, talk shows on which people reveal their deepest secrets, addictions, and marital problems, crime shows where ordinary seeming people turn to murderer. People love drama. In a movie, they do not want to watch people sit around and talk about their problems. They want to see the problems as they unfold. A movie is a series of conflicts, and each scene must have a conflict at its heart.

The Conflict In Kids' Movies

Even movies for children have conflict, sometimes many of them, and some are about serious issues. In *Rio*, Blue the bird is taken from the wild at an early age and raised as a house pet. When he finds himself back in the wild, he is unable to fly to get away from poachers who want to trap him again. In *Beauty and the Beast*, the Beast keeps Belle as his prisoner until they fall in love. In *Aladdin*, a thief masquerades as a prince and courts a princess as he hides his true identity. In *The Incredibles*, Mr. Incredible is forced to retire due to the legal liability involved in being a superhero.

If you are having a hard time identifying the conflict in each scene, consider what is motivating each character. What does each person come into the scene wanting and what can they achieve or gain from this scene? In real life, desire and need motivates people. Your characters similarly have desires and needs they want to fulfill. To get the most authentic portrait of them, know what they want at each moment in the story. As they interact, this desire will be foremost in their mind, even if they try to hide it. They might have a larger motivation in the movie, but consider what they want in each specific scene. It might be something as simple as being in a rush and wanting to get to work without being late. Consider the mood and mindset of each of the characters as they come into the scene. If your protagonist has had a long, stressful day at work, he or she is not going to act the same as if he or she has just woken up fresh from a full night's sleep.

In the "show me the money" scene from *Jerry Maguire*, the conflict between Jerry and his client, Rod, is obvious. Jerry wants to get Rod off the phone as fast as possible in order to call his other clients and save them from being poached by Bob Sugar. Rod wants to air all of his grievances while he has his agent's attention. The conflict makes what is a necessary piece of business — Jerry losing all his clients — a memorable scene.

On the index card from *Getting Out of Grossville*, Emma finds out about the manager position, and Elaine spots a guy she likes. The conflict that comes into this situation can be between the girls, between them and the customers, or between one of them and their boss. It might be more interesting if the conflict comes between the two of them. So let's say the conflict is this:

Emma wants quiet so she can hear all the details about the position, and Elaine is too busy arguing with a customer to care.

This conflict leads us to draw different conclusions than this one would:

Emma wants Elaine to help with the long line of customers, but Elaine only wants to stare at the new baker.

The first conflict would lead us to think Elaine is not too great at her job, has a bad attitude or a nasty temper, or maybe is hungover. The second conflict might lead us to think Elaine is man crazy, the type of girl who puts love in front of everything, including her friends and her job. Written another way, it could also show that love has struck Elaine for the first time. Whatever you decide the conflict will be, think about the different ways it can influence the action in the scene. You also will need to keep this in mind as you write the scene's dialogue.

Creating the Board

You can use any size bulletin board that works in the space you have and accommodates your cards. The standard size (18 X 24) works well if you have enough wall space for it. Thumbtacks are easiest to move the cards around. Tape or adhesive can wear off, and if all the cards fall off the board in the middle of the night, that means a big headache for you the next day. Once you are done writing, you can take the cards down, stack them in order, put a rubber band around them, and store them anywhere. If you need to consult them when you revise the movie, you can pull them out and flip directly to the ones you need.

The four cards you have reserved as title cards should say Act One, Act Two, Act Two, and Act Three. You can place these at the far left-hand side of the board as the rows begin:

Act One: The scenes from the beginning to plot point one.

Act Two: This row runs from the beginning of Act Two to the midpoint.

Act Two: This row runs from the midpoint to the end of Act Two.

Act Three: The scenes that happen from the beginning of Act Three to the end of the movie.

Once the cards are ready, you can affix them to the board in the order they fall in, from left to right. Certain cards will go in a definite place on the board. The end of act one should be at the end of the first row, which should be about ten cards long. The fun second act scenes that help to round out your story can go anywhere in the two middle rows. The climax should be right around the end of the bottom row. The midpoint should be at the end of row two. You might find that there are holes, or places where the action does not quite come together the way it needs to. For example, your board might have these two cards:

EXT-RAMONA'S HOUSE-DAY
Ramona and Jane bicker as they get into the car.
Ramona: frustrated ↓ angry ↑
Jane: calm ↓ angry ↑

Followed by:

EXT-CURB-DAY
Ramona hits Felipe with her car as he crosses the street.
Ramona: angry ↑ horrified ↑
Felipe: happy ↑ injured ↓

Is Ramona distracted by her argument with Jane? Was Felipe not watching where he was going? Do you need more scenes to set this up, or can you include all this information in the second scene before Ramona makes impact with Felipe?

If you have space to add extra cards there, then great. If not, you can try combining scenes to open up some room. Maybe the scenes combine into the second scene, like this:

INT-RAMONA'S CAR-DAY
Ramona and Jane bicker.
Ramona hits Felipe with her car as he crosses the street.
Ramona: frustrated ↓ horrified ↑
Jane: calm ↓ scared ↑
Felipe: happy ↑ injuredy ↓

Remember at this stage, you can allow yourself a little flexibility, as your plans surely will change as you write. You are trying to make a framework for your story, but you also can allow yourself to indulge in your creativity.

Some movies are criticized for being too episodic, a fancy term that means the movie's scenes feel like they do not build toward anything. They do not gain momentum or build tension. The scenes almost seem as though they can be taken out of order, replaced in a different way, and still make sense. To avoid this effect, as you look over the cards, make sure that each scene topples into the next, like a row of dominos. The events of each card should depend on the events of the previous card. Here is an example from Emma's story. We have already discussed this card:

INT-GROCERY STORE-DAY
Emma finds out about the manager position.
Elaine sees the new baker for the first time.

The next card should follow the action of this card. So, we could have a scene that develops the new relationship between Elaine and the new guy, or a scene where Emma tells Elaine of her intentions to apply for the manager position. But just because this scene follows the action of the previous one, does not mean it can only contain the people in the previous scene. We are not limited to just Emma, Elaine, the manager, customers, and the new baker. We can pull in some of the other characters to advance another of the movie's plotlines. What if this scene was next?

INT-EMMA'S HOUSE-NIGHT
Emma tells Sarah she wants the manager job.
Sarah tells her not to get her hopes up.
Emma and Sarah get into a shouting match.

This brings in Sarah, advancing the subplot about her alcoholism, and a subplot about Emma and Sarah's relationship. It also could strengthen Emma's resolve to get the job and prove her mother wrong.

The closer you can get to this in your screenplay, the better off you will be. Knowing what to write next should make the process much easier. Each scene should motivate the viewer to watch the next one. The scenes should move easily at about the same pace. For example, if you have ten cards in the Act One row and only six in the second row, your second act might be off to a slow start. This dip in pacing can be intentional. The pacing might slow down in certain parts, such as during a romance story line, but even then, the action needs to keep moving, and the story still needs to be moving forward.

Think of the emotional notes your characters are opening and closing the scenes on. If they close one scene sad, and the next scene they start out happy, the audience might find it jarring, or they might find it a nice change of pace. If they spend three scenes in a row depressed, that might kill the energy and momentum your script had going up to that point. The emotional state of your protagonist is the most important, as he or she is the character the audience identifies with. If the protagonist is getting battered and bruised, your audience is as well. Is this part of your plan to help the audience root for the protagonist on their journey?

Repeat Locations

In real life, we go to the same places over and over again, and none of them are really that interesting. Work. Home. School. Gas station. The gym. If you are trying to make your movie realistic, keeping to these locations might help you achieve that. But it can also make your movie boring and visually static. After all, people go to the movies to get away from real life. They want to see something extraordinary happen — as long as it makes sense to the story line and is well explained. If you paid the ever-increasing price of a ticket and watched people sit at a coffee shop and talk for two hours, you might be a little miffed. You can turn on your TV and see people doing ordinary things five nights a week for free.

Seeing your characters in the same location every time might give the sense of home and community you were hoping for, or you might decide you would rather have more varied locations to make the movie visually dynamic. What do you think would make the movie more interesting? Where would you like to see your characters? And what will help contribute to the overall tone you want in your movie? If your movie is a sad, emotional drama, maybe having your characters on a ferryboat on a gray, dreary day will help give it the overall mood it needs. If yours is a lighthearted summer comedy, add some outdoor locations where your characters can soak up the sun and interact with each other in different ways. The same way you might try a new activity with your friends, put your characters in a new situation and see if they have fun. Or perhaps the venture outside their comfort zone is a disaster for them, but a funny and interesting scene for the audience to watch. If you hope to make each location symbolic, make sure it appears often enough to register with viewers.

Anticipating and Resolving Problems in Your Screenplay

Your board cannot tell the future, but it can shed some light on your story line's possible shortcomings. You can anticipate certain things from looking at your board. For example, you can see problems that arise in the screenplay, where you might have had difficulty coming up with the next scenes to make the story logical. Parts of the board might be missing cards or have a thin premise holding them together. If each subplot does not have a beginning, middle, and end, now is the time to add them to the cards or discard them. You might have too many cards or not enough. You also can look for patterns you would like to change or reinforce in the screenplay. In *Working Girl*, Tess is seen taking the ferry from Staten Island into Manhattan three times. Each time, she is at a different point in her journey. You can use a callback like this to show your hero's progress.

Setups

As you look at the story cards, you have an opportunity to make sure that your setups are paid off. Every situation you leave unresolved or open ended in the beginning of the movie should get resolved at some point, even if it is much later on. The audience is smart enough to remember the booby trap that is loaded and waiting for your character, and if the character does not fall into it, not only will the audience feel cheated, but you will have wasted time in your screenplay on a story line that goes nowhere.

An easy way to make sure the setups are in place is to look at the later scenes at the climax and ending of the movie. Look at what needs to take place in order for the ending to work, and then trace it back and make sure the situation is set up properly. If your protagonist is going to steal his best friend's gun and shoot the villain at the climax, make sure the best friend shows him where the gun is hidden in a scene before the climax.

Make sure every character arcs

Although the protagonist's arc is most important, every character in your movie is going on a journey, and each journey has to make sense. Maybe you are only going to show a few points of the journey, and that is okay. Minor characters do not have to steal the show. But make sure the scenes you are showing contribute to at least one character's journey, with its own beginning, middle, and end. The villains in your story might not have as much of a journey, or they might undergo a more subtle change, and that is all right. As in life, not everyone matures at the same rate, and every experience does not affect everyone the same way. One example of an antagonist who changes during a movie is Vivian Kensington, the girl Elle Woods initially views as her enemy in *Legally Blonde*. When they meet, Vivian is stuck up, mean, and planning to marry Elle's ex-boyfriend. As Elle grows and changes throughout the movie, Vivian comes to respect her and view her as an equal. By the end of the movie, Vivian and Elle have become best friends.

You might find it hard to describe each character's change in a way that makes it clear to the audience that the character has changed but that does not change who the character is so much that the audience finds it hard to believe. Remember that they are learning from the experiences described in your story. They do not necessarily have to change every aspect of their lives. Think about how the story you are telling directly affects them. What did they learn from this experience? What will they take away from it? Do not try to convince the audience the secondary characters are completely changed nor changed the same way the protagonist has. It is enough to show that the transformation of the protagonist has influenced them. At the end of *My Big Fat Greek Wedding*, Toula's and Ian's contrary families seem to have opened up to each other. Toula's father makes a touching toast welcoming the Millers at the wedding reception, and the Millers get up and dance to a Greek number with Toula's family. There is even a comedic moment in the middle of the movie when Toula's cousins ask if Ian has any eligible brothers for them even though they know he is not Greek.

Let's add a secondary character to *Getting Out of Grossville*, Emma's mother Sarah, who lives with her children in the home they grew up in. Sarah has been sober for many years by attending meetings and mentoring other people, but lately she is having trouble resisting temptation. Sarah's is a serious story that could easily take over and become a main plot, but it does not have to take up the whole movie. To go on the journey with her, the audience simply has to understand each point of her journey. So show them the beginning, when she is attending meetings regularly but with a total lack of enthusiasm. Then add the middle: She goes out and buys a bottle of whiskey and just stares at it, and then she hides it in the house. The audience knows that the bottle is there, ticking like a time bomb, waiting for Emma to find it and confront Sarah about it or for Sarah to crack it open. Then make sure you resolve it, either by showing her renewed commitment to her sobriety or by showing her giving in to her demons.

How does this work into the main plot of Emma's journey? Perhaps her mom's alcoholism is what finally pushes Emma to want to get away from home. Maybe Sarah's struggle is what keeps her there, resenting being Mom's guardian but still too afraid to walk away. Perhaps letting the romance character into her world, including her mom, is what will bring them together as a family and give Sarah the courage to dump the whiskey bottle into the sink.

Weaving subplots into the main plot

As you mark the cards to indicate the subplots, you will start to see how each subplot is shaping up. Because each subplot will only have a few scenes in the finished product, the placement is important. The subplots are often what give the audience a break from the more serious tone of the main plot. A subplot can have as few as three or four scenes to tell its whole story, but that simple subplot adds to the overall movie. Your secondary characters and their alternate views on events offer the audience a breath of fresh air, a fresh spin on the story you are telling. They also can help you drive home the main messages of the plot.

There is no hard and fast rule about how many subplots to include or how many scenes related to the subplot should appear in the final screenplay. You do not want the audience to feel the subplot is rushed or unresolved, so take as much time as needed to truly polish the story off.

As the story progresses, you might find the subplots are taking the attention away from the main plot or taking out the tension that you were hoping to create in the main story. You can move scenes, or space them out a little more, to create more of a flow. Make sure the scenes that compose each subplot are balanced throughout the length of the screenplay. After all, they are the subplots and should come second to the main plot.

Scenes that advance the subplot do not have to stand on their own. They can be combined with scenes that contribute to the main plot or scenes from another subplot. Say you have these two cards:

EXT-HIGHWAY 32-DAY

Elaine breaks down on the way to her first date with

the baker.

INT-EMMA'S HOUSE-DAY

Sarah needs a ride to her first gig.

You can combine these to one card, where Elaine is giving Sarah a ride to her gig on the way to the date, and they break down on the side of the road. You could even combine another card, one that contributes to the main plot:

EXT-HIGHWAY-DAY

Emma, late for work, drives by Sarah and Elaine broken

down on the side of the road.

Sarah and Elaine yell for her to stop.

Emma keeps driving.

Now, three of your plotlines are advanced in one scene. The audience sees that Emma is focused on her goal — so focused that she is putting it ahead of helping her friends and family. Sarah and Elaine do not have to say much to let the audience know where they were going and that they are now going to be late. What ultimately can be a short scene will take care of advancing all these stories.

Writing Up the First Draft, Scene by Scene

ow you have your board with its cards neatly summing up each scene. You have your notes on each scene: what should happen, what each character feels, what the conflict within the scene is. All you have to do now is write a couple of pages based on each card and your notes, put the scenes together into your screenplay, and you are all done. Simple, right? But creating your screenplay from your scattered notes, research, and cards is easier said than done.

In addition to entertaining the audience and making them want to continue watching, each scene is a piece of business. It has things to accomplish within the overall movie. This part of the story, when placed within the line of the other scenes, will help the protagonist on his or her journey to get what he or she truly wants. Even if you have room on the board for a few extra cards, do not be tempted to put in scenes that do not add to the main plot.

Here again, your scenes are like dominoes, and the story line is the path they take. If the dominoes are set up in a straight line, it is not as interesting when you knock them down. But if you take a little more time, you can line them up, all around the room, up and down stairs, in turns and curls, and the more intricately you set them up, the more fun it will be to watch when they come tumbling down.

What is a Scene?

As mentioned previously, a scene runs from the moment it starts until the characters leave the location or you decide that it is over. On the page, each time your characters change location, you will begin a new scene with the heading, the same way it appears on the story card.

For example: **EXT-LIGHTHOUSE-DAY.**

When you structure your scenes, you have to think of each as its own mini movie. They have their own conflicts, their own energy. Each scene needs to be as long as it needs to be to convey the important points, but they should not drag on too long. Your characters should not linger and waste valuable screen time. There are no rules as to how long a scene should be, but generally, scenes should last anywhere from a fraction of a page up to a few pages. You might find some scenes in the screenplay need to be a little longer, about five pages. Scenes that long should be a rarity, and you should not have more than two in your screenplay unless the story requires a long climax scene.

Within each scene, something needs to happen to make the story move forward. The scene itself might focus on what is taking place in the characters' lives that day, but the events of the scene have some longer-term effect on the protagonist, the way he or she relates to the other characters, or the events that are going to take place later on. Even if your characters are in a dialogue-heavy scene in which not much action is taking place, the scene needs to be helping the protagonist get to what he or she is truly after. Because your characters are interesting and charming, you might have some great scenes between them that do not move the story forward, but remember, these are the scenes make the movie lose energy and momentum. They pack the movies that make your squirm in your seat and check your cell phone in the theater. If a scene does not move the story forward, you cannot keep it in the movie, no matter how much you like it. Take whatever aspect of this scene you like and apply it to a scene where something happens. If you are in love with the location, place another scene there. If it is a piece of dialogue you like, put it in another scene.

As you prepare to write a scene, look at the description on the card and try to envision the action in your mind. How can you describe what you see happening on the page? Start at the slug line, which is easy enough. Which of your characters are going to start this scene, and what are they doing? Describe this briefly.

INT-RESTAURANT-NIGHT

Emma and Dave are at a Chinese restaurant, having dinner.

Next, explain the elements of the setting. What does the reader need to know about the setup or layout of this particular Chinese restaurant to understand the action?

INT-RESTAURANT-NIGHT

Emma and Dave are at a Chinese restaurant, having dinner. They clearly have been given the worst seat in the house, a small, uneven table right next to the kitchen doors.

When writing the scene, use simple words to convey the description of the scene and the action. Overdone description will slow the reader down. Say things as simply as possible, and use words that could appear in just about anyone's vocabulary.

Take this story card:

INT-EMMA'S HOUSE-DAY
Emma gets up early for work.
Sarah can't sleep.

This scene does not require much dialogue. See the example below:

INT-EMMA'S HOUSE-DAY

Emma walks into the kitchen in her work uniform. Sarah is already at the table, reading the Bible. The morning sun shines through the slats of the blinds.

> EMMA
> You're up early

> SARAH
> Couldn't sleep. What time are you working?

> EMMA
> 7:30. Elaine's picking me up.

> SARAH
> Tell her I said hi.

> EMMA
> I will.

Emma turns to leave, then looks back at Sarah

> EMMA
> (continued)
> Maybe you should check out that meeting on
> Seventy-First and Fifth. They have good donuts at
> that coffee shop on the corner.

> SARAH
> Maybe I will.

Emma puts on her uniform hat and walks out.

Instead of coming out and saying exactly what she means (You're acting weird, and I'm concerned about your sobriety), Emma reminds her mom of the Alcoholics Anonymous meeting held nearby. Sarah's response is fairly neutral and does not give much away about her mental state. The viewer knows there is a conflict here: Emma wants her mom to stay sober, and Sarah is losing the will to stay sober. The scene also has a lot of subtext, words left unsaid, to draw viewers in and pique their curiosity. Why can't Emma come out and say what she means? Obviously there is some history concerning Emma and Sarah's relationship and Sarah's struggle with sobriety. As the story goes on, the viewer can collect more clues to what the history here is. This scene's main purpose advances the subplot about Sarah's sobriety, but it also subtly ties in to the main plot, as Emma is getting ready to go to work.

The scene description should be kept short and simple, with not too many details. As they come in, introduce your characters with a few descriptive words, but make sure you are concentrating more on their physical descriptions and not on their backstories. Remember that nothing that cannot be conveyed on screen should be in the screenplay. Instead of:

> Sarah, 45, Emma's mom, ten years sober, is blond with blue eyes. She carries the demons of her misspent youth with her, in the form of a limp.

This example is better:

> Sarah, 45, is Emma's mom, and it is evident she was once beautiful like her daughter. She twirls an AA coin in her hand as she limps quickly along the sidewalk.

By making the limp something that does not hinder Sarah, it helps the viewer to draw the conclusion that this is an old injury. She already has learned how to compensate for it and work around it. It might come out later that Sarah quit drinking after she injured herself and Emma in a car accident.

When to Pee

The site RunPee (**www.runpee.com**) is a database of moments viewers have deemed missable in movies. The app, available for various platforms, tells you which parts of the movie are not crucial and what you will miss if you run to the bathroom during the action. As you review your movie for scenes that do not matter to the plot, ask yourself, is this the part of the movie that audience members will be leaving in favor of the bathroom?

Building Energy

The action within the scene is important. Scenes can open with energy and a burst of action — often action is the best way to start the scene. The movie *Speed* starts with the SWAT team rescuing a group of people in a booby-trapped elevator. The action gets the viewers into the story right away, while also planting setups — the use of bombs to trap innocent people and terrorize them — that will come back in the story's main plotline.

It also establishes the tense pace that dominates the rest of the movie. Or the scene can start at a place of low energy and build up toward the conflict. This can help to create tension and suspense if you are writing a thriller or horror screenplay. But pace the scene carefully to avoid drawing it out, too. We have all seen the horror movie cliché where the hero comes slowly up the stairs, while the audience knows the killer is in the house. Drawn out perfectly, it creates suspense and makes the viewer squirm. Drawn out too long, it makes the viewer dismiss the scene as overdone and the movie as implausible.

Some movies start right in the midst of a big event, or in the denouement, and then flash back to set the events up. If you begin this way, know that you have to take the audience so far, and get them so involved in the journey, that they all but forget about what they have already seen.

To make the scene more energetic, you can try cutting some off the start of the scene. The action will start faster and draw the audience in. The audience does not need you to tell them everything. They will make logical leaps with you. Let's say you are writing the scene for this card:

INT-GROCERY STORE-DAY
A customer complains about Elaine.
Manager asks Emma to handle it.

The aim of this scene is to show Emma's progress in her job. The manager has trusted her with some responsibility by asking her to resolve the situation. But Emma knows this is also a test to see if she is mature enough to put her friendship with Elaine aside and act as a manager should.

Here is a first draft of the scene:

INT-BAKERY COUNTER-DAY

Elaine stands behind the bakery counter, looking across the rest of the store, as though she is waiting for someone to show up. She is wearing a full face of makeup and jewelry. A customer approaches the counter.

CUSTOMER
Hi. What kind of grains are in the whole grain bread?

ELAINE
The grainy kind.

CUSTOMER
No, really.

ELAINE
They're really grainy.

CUSTOMER
Did you wake up on the wrong side of the bed or something?

ELAINE
Do you have some desire to never wake up again?

CUSTOMER
Did you just threaten me?

INT-BAKERY COUNTER-FIVE MINUTES LATER

Emma comes to around the corner to find the manager standing next to Elaine, who is yelling incoherently at the customer. The customer has picked up a baguette and is swinging it at Elaine.

                          EMMA
                    What's going on?

The customer turns toward Emma, now swinging the baguette
wildly in all directions.

                        CUSTOMER
                  Don't come any closer!

                          EMMA
         Sir, just put the bread down, let's talk about this.

                        CUSTOMER
                  (puts the bread down)
        This woman threatened me! If she isn't fired, I'm
                  never shopping here again.

                        MANAGER
        Sir, I'm the manager here, and I'd be happy to re-
                    solve this for you.

A voice calls for the manager to customer service over the intercom.

                        MANAGER
                      (continued)
        I apologize, sir. I'm going to have to go take care of
        that. But Emma here is one of my best senior staff,
         and I trust her completely to take care of this.

The manager walks away from the bakery counter. As he passes
Emma, he leans over and hisses in her ear.

                        MANAGER
                       Fix this!

As you write the second draft, you might want to cut the first portion of the scene to make the pacing faster and allow yourself more time to deal with the resolution to the situation instead of the setup. In the second draft, you could look at cutting the whole section that occurs between Elaine and the customer and start the scene when Emma comes around the corner. The customer tells us what we missed: Elaine was rude, the situation escalated, and he is now so angry he wants to see her fired. Each scene has to end by resolving the conflict within this part of the story. But a good screenwriter knows how to pique our interest for the next scene as well.

INT-GROCERY STORE-DAY
Emma hears about the manager position.
Elaine sees the new baker for the first time.

The grocery store scene that stems from the above card moves the main plot along by informing Emma, and the audience, about the new position. But coming out of it, our interest is piqued to see if Emma can turn things around and win the manager position. We also should be motivated to see what happens with Elaine and her new friend. How does Elaine's subplot tie into the main plot? Maybe this is the beginning of a distance between the girls that helps Emma see that she is capable of being more independent. Each scene should give the viewer another grain of information, another seed of interest that makes them want to keep watching.

Pacing your film

As you structure your film, consider the overall pace of your movie. Do you want to speed it up? Try cutting the beginnings and ends of your scenes where you can, to make the action happen faster. You do not have to show Emma driving to Elaine's house. When she shows up at the door, breathing heavily, hair frazzled, car keys swinging from one hand, the audience will assume she drove over in a frenzy and ran to the door with urgent news.

Another way to make the plot seem to move faster is adding a time element. Mentioned in Chapter 3, a time element is anything that adds a deadline to the hero's journey. Humanity as we know it is going to meet its end. The protagonist's true love is about to leave town forever. A holiday/wedding/college reunion is coming up soon that the hero has to attend.

This instantly adds tension to the movie. The ticking clock, as it is sometimes called, does not have to be a prominent feature of your film. You do not have to keep referencing it as the story goes on or counting down how much time is left. In the opening minutes of *The Sisterhood of the Traveling Pants*, the girls reveal they will be apart for the summer and they will share a "magical" pair of pants evenly over the summer. The audience knows each of the girls only will have a short time to resolve her story.

A ticking clock automatically gives the movie more of a sense of urgency. The audience knows a deadline is looming and extra pressure is building on the characters. Once the deadline is set, the pace of your movie automatically picks up without you even realizing it.

After you have added a deadline, as you add complications to the second act, you can try making the clock tick faster. This is not as hard to do as it sounds. Plans change all the time. Maybe the grocery store Emma works for has decided they need to get someone much faster than originally planned.

You can relax the tension in the same film by placing a few scenes with no mention of the ticking clock in them together. This gives the audience a rest from the pace you have created and lets them forget about the tension for a while, so when the tension comes back, they are surprised and ready to jump onboard again.

Brainstorming: The ticking clock

Some famous films that feature a time element:

Black Swan: From the start of the movie, we are aware the company is progressing toward a production of *Black Swan*. Without being told, the audience knows that opening night of the ballet will finish the film.

Beauty and the Beast: In this Disney classic, the enchantment put on the beast centers on a magic rose. If the rose dies before the beautiful girl falls in love with him, he will be stuck in his beastly form forever.

Get Him to the Greek: The record company only has a limited time to get drugged up Aldous Snow to the Greek Theater for a career-saving performance.

What Makes a Great Scene?

Think of the scenes you love. What makes them stand out? Why are they remarkable?

The scene at the end of *Say Anything*, where Lloyd stands in the rain in with his boom box. The shower scene from *Pyscho*. The girls getting sick at the bridal store in *Bridesmaids*. These scenes are memorable, each for evoking a different emotion and staying with us long after we see the film. *Say Anything* evokes the craziness of first love. *Psycho* taps into the fear of being surprised at a vulnerable time. *Bridesmaids* makes us laugh with disgust and sympathy.

The best scenes are the ones where things happen. This does not necessarily mean the hero has to be shooting at bad guys or saving the world, but something of consequence needs to be happening. They have action; they matter to the outcome of the story. For example, we all remember the scene in *Pulp Fiction* where the characters discuss the Royale with cheese. Though the dialogue and delivery are what everyone remembers, Jules and Vincent are still moving the story line along as they drive to pick up the briefcase.

Good scenes evoke emotion. They make you laugh or cry. They often are grounded in a truth the viewer can relate to. The scenes that make you cry in movies often do so because they remind you of a past love, an emotional life event, or a relative who has passed away. To keep these scenes from becoming cliché, try to establish the characters and their behavior patterns early on. This will help the viewer understand who they are and accept their behavior. Even in the silliest of movies, the comedy comes from something real happening to the characters. In *There's Something About Mary*, the audience laughs at the things that happen to Ted. But all of these things come about through a journey rooted in emotion: Ted is looking for his long-lost love, Mary. Would the accident with his zipper be as funny if it had not happened on prom night at Mary's house? Silly though it might be, it gives us a premise we can relate to. Through all the gross and improbable things Ted endures to get Mary back in his life, we hang on to the emotional hook: He is doing it for love.

The Business of the Scene

We have all seen a movie in which the characters talk too much. Not enough happens and the talking overwhelms the action. In a scene, the characters need something to do to keep them looking busy. Too many scenes of characters talking to teach other in a coffee shop or restaurant can make the movie seem slow. Instead, they could be going for a walk. Many movies set in New York City have a scene of people walking in Central Park.

Think of your life. You probably spend most of your time with your loved ones handling the business of everyday life: driving from one place to another, cooking, eating, doing dishes, getting dressed, grocery shopping, going to church. Rarely do you sit still and only talk.

Giving the characters something to do makes your job as a screen-writer easier. It gives you a way to show the audience things about your characters instead of telling them. This allows you to use the visual medium to your advantage. Where they are and what they are up to tell us many things about your characters. If your movie is about a teen who is headed down the wrong path, show us why. Instead of having the character's mom yell at her "You're going down the wrong path!" give us a scene in which the teen is shoplifting at the mall at 10 a.m. when she should be at school. This allows the audience to use their own perception to understand the character. Maybe they will think she is a bad seed, or maybe they will simply think this is a normal part of adolescence. Either way, they are thinking about the movie and forming an opinion on it because you are allowing them the room to view and digest it, instead of spoon-feeding them what they should think via the speeches of other characters. Now, you can use the dialogue to progress the story instead of using it to explain things to us.

Scene Business

Some ideas for what your characters might be doing as they talk:

- Changing a tire or the oil in the car instead of driving in the car

- Cooking a meal together instead of simply sitting at a restaurant

- Doing one another's nails instead of sitting at the nail salon

- Going through their clothes and choosing items to give to charity instead of shopping for new clothes

- Riding bicycles or walking instead of driving somewhere

Conveying the right message

Let's say that your index card reads:

INT-EDUARDO'S APARTMENT-DAY

Gloria begs Eduardo not to get married.

In this scene, your protagonist, Eduardo, is preparing to leave town to go to his wedding, and his mother, Gloria, has stopped by to beg him to reconsider. Let's say you want to convey that Eduardo is an independent man, not a mama's boy, and that although his loves his mother, he will do as he pleases. Already, by showing Eduardo at his own apartment, we know that he is not under his mother's thumb. Perhaps Gloria mentions some changes to his décor he has never made, despite her repeated nagging. This can show that Eduardo indulges his mother but does not really take her suggestions seriously. In the end, he walks out to go to the wedding, which shows his character more than anything.

Devising activities characters do together can also show something about their relationship as well. Two coworkers having lunch together do not have the same relationship as two best friends huddled together in grief after one loses a parent. Two characters committing a crime together have an implied level of trust in one another. Maybe you can surprise your audience with how little they know about each other as the story progresses. The same goes for a man and woman being intimate unless the location of the scene is a nightclub bathroom or anonymous hotel room. A boss and his employee have a certain type of relationship, bound by the rules of the workplace and the expectations society has for two people in these positions. A husband and wife, behind closed doors, are expected to hold nothing back from each other. When we see them in this setting, it makes us think we are getting the real, unvarnished truth about their lives unless we find out they are having some relationship issue or being deceitful with each other.

All of these parts of the scene help you to convey what you want the audience to know. Let each scene be a peek into the lives of your characters, so your viewers can get to know them.

Setting The Tone Of Your Scenes

The director, set designers, and cinematographer will have a lot of influence over the final look of your movie. Yet as the screenwriter, you can influence the tone of your scenes. The locations that you choose, the lighting and conditions you describe, and even the music contribute to the mood of your scenes.

The lighting can create a mood. A daytime scene, in a sunny yellow kitchen with lots of windows, sets a happy, cheerful mood. As the screenwriter, you have a limited number of words to get that mood across. Using words such as bright, calm, clear to describe a summer day, or bright colors like green, yellow or orange in the room can help to get that mood across. A darker sky, with shadows cast all around, sets a gloomier tone. The same scene can be influenced greatly by the weather conditions you describe.

The activity your characters are engaging in can influence the mood of a scene. Dancing, laughing, and playing with each other can create an infectious sort of laughter between the characters and into the audience. Think of the way you and your friends interact, and use those friendly gestures in the script. Things like giggles, belly laughs, play fighting with

each other, or singing a song from childhood tell the audience something about the level of comfort that exists between the characters. They can help you set a fun, silly, or nostalgic mood.

Surprising the Viewer with What They Already Know

The audience might see the end coming for your characters. Though you will do your best to make the story original and fresh, some parts of the movie will be obvious to some viewers. If yours is a love story in which one of the lovers has hidden something from the other, the audience knows the lie is going to come back to bite them. In a thriller, if the hero has managed to run away from a tormentor, we know the bad guy is going to show up again as soon as the hero manages to find happiness in a new life.

Besides what they can guess, the audience might have gained a superior position, the term for when the audience knows more than the characters do. The job of the screenwriter then becomes making the audience forget what they know, so they can be surprised. Let them get so swept up in the journey that they forget all about what is coming.

Just as you would in real life, you can change the topic and avoid the main plotline for a moment. Delve into a subplot for a few scenes, so the recent developments can have a few moments to fade away. Keep the narrative moving quickly so the new action developing on screen keeps the viewer from dwelling on what just happened. By doing this, you can surprise them with ideas and plot points they figured out in the beginning.

Putting the Cherry on Top

Some scenes end with a little kick, a punch line, or a burst of action, known in the movie business as a button. Adding a button puts the period on the end of the sentence written by your scene — or sometimes an exclamation point. Here's a simple button:

INT-KITCHEN-DAY

Wife is putting freshly baked cookies on a cooling rack. Husband comes in and tries to steal one.

> WIFE
>
> No, these are for my bake sale. Go away!

> HUSBAND
>
> Come on, just one.

> WIFE
>
> No. I said no! Get out!

Husband leaves. Wife finishes with the cookies and walks away. Husband runs back in and reaches out to steal one.

> WIFE
>
> (off screen)
>
> I said no!

Husband slumps away.

The button gives the scene a definite ending point. It adds a little point of levity to the scene. It also can provide a new, fresh energy to take the audience into the next scene.

An example of a button in *Waiting to Exhale* is when Gloria has walked across the street to meet her handsome new neighbor. As she begins to walk back after their conversation, she says to herself, "I hope he's not watching me walk away." She then turns, waves at the neighbor, and continues the walk back to her house, saying to herself, "He is." The comment adds a little laugh and takes us out of the scene with good energy.

Buttons can be difficult to write, but worth putting some thought into. A button can make a simple scene memorable; for example, the scene in *Pretty Woman* when Julia Roberts goes back to the Rodeo Drive boutique she was chased out of the day before to tell the saleslady off. Dressed in a modest suit, she sweeps in with shopping bags in hand, passes by a saleslady who offers to help, and confronts the woman who refused to wait on her. What we remember more than ten years later is what Julia says to the woman as she sweeps back out: "Big mistake. Big. Huge. I have to go shopping now."

The button is what makes this scene so satisfying. It adds comedy and a certain satisfaction to the scene. Most important, it ends the scene decisively. There is nothing else for the clerk to say, so she does not try. Also, we as the audience are ready to check out of this scene and head into the next one.

Talking the Talk

ou sit in front of your computer screen. You have planned the scene so well, you already know who will be there, why they will be there, and what is on their mind. You know where the scene begins and where it needs to go. Yet, as you sit there, one thing is eluding you. What are these people going to say? And how are they going to say it?

Writing the way people talk is exceedingly difficult. Some people take time to formulate the right way to say things, practice them over time, and fine-tune their comments into the perfect opening line, the joke that steals everyone's attention at a cocktail party. Their brains, influenced by their tastes and experiences, filter the words they choose. Other people speak freely without thinking, not worried about consequences until they happen. You must decide each of your characters' style, the way he or she speaks, the image he or she hopes to project, and his or her motivation in this particular scene before you craft the dialogue.

Dialogue needs to have a purpose in advancing the plot. But it cannot state this purpose too plainly. As the writer, you now find yourself and your characters at cross-purposes. You, as the screenwriter, want the characters to convey your clever dialogue, the plot you have carefully devised. Yet, your characters have their own voices, their own agendas, and their own lives that have nothing to do with your narrative. They will want to talk about those things.

The magic comes in finding the way to make the words your characters speak authentic to them but tailored to advance your script. You have to find a way to make the words they say convey more than just the words themselves.

Once again, knowing your characters will help you in this part of the writing. Even if your characters are not the types to think before they speak, you have to consider their mindset before the words slip out of their mouths. What do they want out of the scene? Maybe it is a tangible desire, or maybe they simply want some peace and quiet. What does each character need to get out of the scene? This is a different question than the first. Maybe one needs to get $5 from another character to buy food. You must decide, based on your knowledge of that character and the one he or she is bumming money from, what he or she needs to say in order to get it.

What is the dynamic between the characters in the scene? How close is the relationship? How much do they want to reveal and how quickly? All of these questions influence the dynamic between the characters and the way they talk to each other.

Creating Distinctive Voices

As you begin writing the dialogue for your screenplay, you might find each of the characters has the same voice, and the voice is yours. It is hard to talk like someone else. As you write the first draft, the most important thing is to get your idea on the page. In the effort to do this, you might end up writing the dialogue of each character in the same way: the way you would say it. After you finish writing the scene and you read over your first draft, you can try to make each voice distinctive and let the personality of each of your characters come through.

Knowing about your characters, as discussed in earlier chapters, is important when you try to craft the dialogue. Each person has a different vocabulary and prefers certain words. This vocabulary comes from reading, school, traveling, seeing and being exposed to different things. Their personality and upbringing will affect their speech patterns and the way they present themselves to the world. Their age will affect what words they choose. Their hometown will influence the slang they use. The rhythms of their speech might also vary based on their background. Stay true to each character's personality in the way he or she talks. A character that wants to appear worldly might avoid words that give away his or her small-town backgrounds at any cost.

How much they speak is different. Some people prefer the sound of their own voices. Others say little and would rather listen. Still others are shy or scared in public but are quite chatty with friends and family. In a screenplay, all your dialogue should be short and to the point. Still, you can find a way to incorporate someone who speaks in as few words as possible against someone who likes to talk. This can be used to comedic effect if a character that does not say much suddenly gives a long speech. Or the opposite can happen, in which a long-winded person is suddenly rendered speechless.

Your character's confidence levels, how they present themselves to the world, and the image they try to craft for themselves come into play here. Ronald Reagan and Barack Obama are known as great speakers. They share some traits all good public speakers share: confidence, voice control, and charisma. But they are completely different as people. Just because your characters have a few traits in common or share a common interest does not mean they should turn into carbon copies of one another. Think about what binds them together, but also what sets them apart.

In certain situations, your characters might consciously talk in a similar way or a similar pattern. Teenagers talk in the same slang to fit in. If your character is a gang member, he or she might have a certain slang the whole gang uses to conceal their plans from eavesdroppers. People in the same profession might talk in work lingo. Even then, they will use the same words but not necessarily put them together the same way.

Think about the preferred phrases of each of your characters. These do not have to be catchphrases or sound bites. It can be as simple as whether he or she is likely to say "No" versus "No, ma'am." Is he or she the affectionate kind, who calls everyone honey or baby? These verbal patterns can distinguish his or her way of speaking from the other characters.

Nonverbal cues

What your characters say with their body language is just as important as what they say with words. You do not want to write a long series of stage directions, as you have to leave some of this up to the actors. Still, you can take some time to think about the body language of your characters, how they carry themselves, the way they move. All of this plays into the characters' personalities, communication styles, and confidence levels. It helps you develop a full personality for the character instead of making him or her stereotypical.

If your character is a womanizer who flirts with every woman he sees, the stereotype that comes to mind is an overly confident guy who approaches every woman with his swagger and pickup lines. But if your hero is more of a geek type who uses his technical savvy to come on to girls, his body language is not going to fit that stereotype. He might be less aggressive and more soft-spoken. His approach might be less direct but with the same result. Your job now is to paint the picture of how he gets there.

Verbal Sparring

Your characters are entering into each scene with the conflict between them standing in the way of what they want. They are going in to do battle, and their words are the only weapons they have. Perhaps a scene is not that serious; maybe it is just a minor disagreement between friends. But to make your dialogue compelling, you have to think that each scene, each conflict is serious. Think about what is on each character's mind before he or she speaks, their inner dialogue. Is the voice inside begging to shout at another character? Or is the hero restraining himself from telling the boss just what he thinks? Knowing this inner struggle can help you better express the outer struggle.

As they fight for what they want, one character might lead the conversation and the other might follow. The character that leads might be questioning the other to get some information. Or they might be teasing the other person, enjoying the power of knowing something secret.

INT-LIVING ROOM-DAY

RUTH

I talked to Jack.

LANCE

Why would you do that?

RUTH

Jack says that he saw you on Friday.

LANCE

Jack doesn't know what he saw.

RUTH

Where were you on Friday?

LANCE

Where I said I was the last time you asked.

One might have to probe while the other reluctantly gives bits and pieces of information.

INT-LIVING ROOM-DAY

LANCE

Did you see Jack?

RUTH

We just talked.

LANCE

On the phone?

RUTH

We just talked.

LANCE

Did you see him?

RUTH

I just wanted to know the truth, once and for all.

LANCE

Did you go to his house?

RUTH

I never would've had to go if you'd told me the
truth!

Like a piece of well-composed music, your scene is made up of beats. These are the points where the energy shifts from one character to the other. Identifying these beats and counting them can be helpful to your writing process. You also can identify the energy that goes with each beat. As this energy shift happens, the characters will speak to each other differently. Their attitudes will change. In the first version of the scene, Ruth has the power. She is persistent, and sure of herself. In the second scene, Lance has the power. He has become more persistent, while Ruth is defensive and reticent. Try to pinpoint the moment in the scene that the power between the characters in the scene shifts. Examine how that shift in power changes the mindset of each character in the scene.

Subtext

In your screenplay as in life, the things left unsaid can be just as significant as those that come out into the open. Your characters might not evolve to the point where they can express themselves fully to their loved ones. The wounds that have been in place for years might not heal totally in the span of your screenplay. Secrets might simmer, unexposed, just under the surface of the story. Subtext is the part of the conversation that pricks your ears up as you listen, the part that makes you think something is up.

As a viewer, you know when something important is being left unsaid between two characters. Subtext helps create tension and suspense in a scene. By keeping your characters from saying everything that is on their minds, it helps to draw the viewer in to the story line and make him or her want to continue watching. It makes the scene more interesting for the viewer. However, you still need to consider these unspoken words, so you can express them in other ways.

Consider how you might act if your boss at a new job called you by another name. You might not want to say anything and risk embarrassing him or her. But you might show that you are offended. You might be rude or sarcastic for the rest of the day. Perhaps you would go out of your way to drop your name into conversation, hoping he or she will realize on his or her own.

In Emma's story, her mother's alcoholism is no doubt a sore subject. Emma might refer to one of the times her mother let her down because she was too busy drinking. But she probably will reference it obliquely. Instead of saying "I wish you hadn't missed my swim meets because you were too drunk to drive," she would most likely just say, "I wish you hadn't missed my swim meets." The other part of the sentence is left unsaid, but the unspoken words hang between them creating weight and tension between the two characters.

If Emma is passive aggressive in the way she expresses herself, she might say, "Anna Thompson's mom and sister went to every swim meet. They even made signs on poster board." This is a more complete, specific memory that paints a more vibrant picture and more subtext. Now the viewer can start to imagine a younger Emma, disappointed as she watches for her mom to arrive, hurt as she watches her teammate with the perfect family. Emma does not have to explain because the audience understands how much that would hurt a teenage girl.

Your characters are only human after all. Though they might have good intentions, they will be flawed, or they should be if you hope to make them convincing. You can expect them to be honest with everyone all the time. You have to find a way to make their real intentions and meanings come through the words they speak about other topics. If your dialogue is too on the nose, no one will believe it.

Again, nonverbal cues will help convey the subtext. The look on the character's face might betray him or her. They might force themselves to say something but their faces might not look happy about it. The hardest part of telling a lie, selling a truth you do not believe in, is making it believable. Your body language may betray the truth and make the lie less believable.

Going back to the verbal sparring, when there is tension between two people, they hold themselves differently. The stress is apparent in their faces, and they might twist and turn in their seats uncomfortably.

Words get in the way

Too much dialogue can hamper a script. In real life, especially these days when we spend most of our time texting and emailing, actual words exchanged between people are few and far between. Sometimes in television and the movies, people speak in long soliloquies and no one interrupts them. But in real life, if you tried to speak to your family about your feelings for three minutes, you probably would be interrupted within the first 45 seconds. Have your characters be as direct with each other as they can. If your mother asks you if you would like a drink, would you really say, "Yes, mother, I would"? More likely, you would say, "Yes," or "Yes, please," or maybe you would just nod. If you are under the age of 20, you might say "Whatever."

Characters in movies speak fewer words because their time is so limited. Your characters only have a few words to make an impression. You do not want to waste those words on things like "What did you have for lunch?" or "Where did you buy that sweater?"

Back to the scene from *Getting Out of Grossville*. Emma and Elaine are good friends, and as is often the case with good girl friends, they probably have a shorthand. They probably do not address each other by name often. Emma would not say to Elaine "I got a ride from my brother Marcus," because Elaine doubtlessly knows who Marcus is.

Sometimes, you can work a scene on nonverbal clues alone, without even needing to resort to dialogue. Think of the concluding image in *The Godfather*. We see Michael, framed by the capos, elevated to the status of Don. We see Kay as she watches, the realization of what her husband has become striking her.

Imagine if they had spoken that whole scene, and the implications of it:

MICHAEL
I'm still the guy you married!

KAY
No, you're not! You're the Godfather!

MICHAEL
Am not!

KAY
Are too! I saw the capos kissing your ring.

Sometimes, dialogue has less of an impact than an image. The audience is smart enough to absorb the implications of Kay's and Michael's nonverbal cues in the last shot. This is also a good way to keep the audience thinking about the movie long after it is over.

The same things that would be difficult for you to say aloud can be difficult for your characters. I want a divorce. I love you. I have cancer. These are not typically things characters yell out or reveal at a first meeting. This is why your scenes need to be crafted in a certain order. The audience needs to see the character preparing to reveal him or herself, letting his or her guard down. The characters have to build a rapport with one another. The conversations they have before the movie's climax should show this relationship forming or growing closer.

Exposition

Expository dialogue is designed to inform the viewer about something they need to know or remind them of something. For example, in a heist movie, the audience needs to understand how the caper is supposed to go, just in case it goes wrong, which it almost always will. However, listening to someone explain something is not the most interesting thing to watch. It also can make your characters seem less authentic. You might need to craft the scene containing the long expository explanation with something exciting going on in the background to pique the visual interest of the audience, even as they are listening to the boring exposition. Often, movies that center on a crime caper have this problem. As the technical elements of the crime have to be explained, exactly how the safe will be cracked and the treasure hidden, some visual distractions are offered to keep you looking.

For example, let's say that while researching *Getting Out of Grossville*, you speak to workers and managers at different grocery stores in your area to see how the day-to-day process goes. One of the managers tells you a story about how one time, after prying open a crate of fresh bananas, a large tarantula came crawling out. This is something that might lend itself well to a movie.

So you decide you have a necessary scene with exposition about how the new manager will be chosen. Just before this scene, you offer a scene where a spider Emma just found in a banana crate gets away. Now Emma finds herself in the manager's office watching the spider crawl all over the manager's chair, but she is too scared to say anything. The audience will be busy following the spider along with Emma; they will hear the exposition but they will not be put to sleep by it. As the eye is looking at something else, the brain can be tricked into listening.

If you feel the audience needs reminding about a scene or an event that happened at the beginning or that was talked about earlier in the script, think of a way you can call back the incident. Let's say that in your movie, the protagonist is Annie, whose house burned down in a fire two weeks ago. To give the audience some idea of how much time has passed, you want to bring this up. Tuck this old business into some new business. For example, Annie's mom might inquire into the status of her insurance claim, as any concerned mom might do.

ANNIE'S MOM
Have you spoken to the insurance company?

ANNIE
Not yet.

ANNIE'S MOM
Why not? It's been two weeks

ANNIE
I just can't deal with it yet

The dialogue in this scene reminds the viewer of how long ago the fire was, but it also accomplishes new business of pushing the story forward. It shows us a little about Annie's and her mother's characters.

Chapter 10

Emphasizing the Important Parts

Every page in your screenplay should be the best you can make it. Each scene should grab the reader and keep him or her interested. But certain parts require special attention. Your opening needs to do as much as it can to get every viewer invested in the story and paying attention. The end of your movie needs to leave the viewer satisfied and informed. In addition to those parts, Hollywood legend has it that agents and readers only read certain pages of each screenplay. Though most readers claim this is not true, some admit they pay more attention to certain pages than others.

The Beginning

How you open your screenplay is an important decision. You will want to set the tone and pace of the film, but you also want to get to the action as fast as possible. Starting the movie in a way that will grab the audience's attention is important. Whether this is verbal action, like an argument between two of your characters, or physical action, like a chase scene, can help set the tone for what else to expect in the movie. *How to start your scene was mentioned in more detail in Chapter 6.*

Using a crash, bang, or boom at the opening of your movie might not work if yours is a quieter film or a family feature. You want to pique the audience's curiosity without leading them down the wrong path. The questions the opening image brings up should be those that will be answered over the course of the movie.

Introducing your movie

Despite your desire to grab the audience, make sure your opening is tailored to the tone and style of your movie. The opening image of your film should draw the audience in and make them curious about this movie specifically. Using an image of an exciting event or beautiful location does not help unless it is relevant to the story. The Grand Canyon at sunset is a beautiful sight, but if your story is about a doctor who just happens to live nearby, does it make sense to open with it? Will that prepare the audience for your film, which primarily shows the doctor at his clinic, home, and gym? If the doctor is going to come to the Grand Canyon at some point in the story and have a realization about life, then this location can become a symbol, a setup of sorts. After seeing it in the opening, the audience will be intrigued to see it again, and make the connection between the doctor's journey and the location.

Your protagonist is the audience's car on the roller coaster. Subconsciously, once they identify who the protagonist is, they know the ride is about to start. They will connect with this person throughout the movie. The sooner the hero can get on screen, the better. If he or she appears as part of a group, try to distinguish him or her in some way. At the start of *Miss Congeniality,* a quick scene shows us Grace Hart as a child, a tough tomboy who tries to help others and only gets ridicule in exchange for her efforts. As we jump forward into Grace's future, the audience lands smack in the middle of an FBI sting. There is no voice-over or anyone who says, "Hey, Grace." But the audience sees the one woman on a team of men, a frumpy looking girl who once again tries to help and gets no thanks for her efforts. They know right away that this is Grace, grown up but still the same. Likewise, if the hero is going to have a helpful sidekick, try to introduce him or her early on as well. Establish the rapport between the reflection and the hero. Try to give the audience some idea of how well these two know each other.

Flipping to Page Ten

Page ten is one of the pages rumored be most important. The exact reason why can vary: some want to make sure the main story is kicking off on time. Others use this page as a yardstick for how well paced the rest of the movie will be. Another reason is limited time. The reader would rather jump to page ten, by which all the foundation should be laid and they can jump in at the interesting part.

By page ten, all of the setup should be in place, the audience should have a picture of the protagonist's life, and the incident, the one that will change the hero's life forever, should be taking place. If your scenes are about two pages long, that gives you five scenes to set up the story. It might not seem like much, but it is equivalent to ten minutes of screen time. The action needs to start unraveling, particularly if you want to resolve everything without having to rush.

To set up Emma's story, you might draft the following five scenes:

Opening scene: Emma and Elaine at work, slacking off. The scene shows Emma's current job, her attitude, and her friendship with Elaine.

Scene 2: Emma throws the brunch for her friend. This scene highlights how small the town Emma lives in really is, and how most people in the town marry and start families at a young age.

Scene 3: Emma hears her friends gossiping about her. Here, the audience sees that Emma's friends are insincere, and her friendships based on superficial things.

Scene 4: Emma tries to confide in her mom but gets no help there. The scene shows how fragile Emma's relationship with Sarah is and could even introduce Sarah's alcoholism.

Scene 5: Emma goes out and gets drunk to deal with her bad day. The audience sees that Emma does not really deal with her problems.

By page ten, Emma is returning to work, hungover and sour, where she will hear about the manager position in the scene we outlined earlier.

The MacGuffin

A MacGuffin is a classic term for a plot device that propels the story line forward. It is something that everyone in the movie wants and tries to get at some point. In some films, the MacGuffin is not a tangible thing. It can be fame or respect. Other writers choose to make the MacGuffin visual, something for the audience to hold onto. The story somewhat revolves around this MacGuffin, with characters wanting it more and more and sometimes competing with each other to get it.

Alfred Hitchcock, the noted filmmaker, made the term MacGuffin famous. For example, the briefcase in *Pulp Fiction* has been described as a MacGuffin. Toted throughout the film's events, the mysterious briefcase is at the heart of the screenplay. The briefcase, its contents, or the mysterious glow are never explained, but the other characters in the movie try to get it. The MacGuffin continues to propel the story forward, yet it might become less urgent as the story goes forward. Once the briefcase is delivered to Marsellus, we do not know what comes of it. MacGuffins are often left open to interpretation and are not always explained to the viewer. Sometimes they are not even thought out in detail.

Closing the Story

Your cards should give you some ideas of how your movie will end. But even with these cards, ending your movie can be difficult. Getting all of the plots wrapped up into a cohesive ending is one thing. But making that conclusion, all that business necessary to resolve all the conflicts seem interesting or funny, is a different thing altogether.

The end of a movie comprises two real parts: the climax, where the main story line is resolved, and the ending, the last scenes of the movie before the end fades to black.

The climax

The movie's main story line is resolved at the climax, which is not the end of the movie. The climax takes place shortly before the movie fades to black, about ten minutes, or ten pages before. The climax of Emma's story would be the announcement of who will get the manager position. That moment resolves the central journey. Yet the movie cannot fade to black the second Emma finds out if she has won or lost the position. There is still business to resolve: letting the audience know what happens between Emma and her love interest, if Elaine and the new baker ever get a romance started, how Sarah fares with her alcoholism.

Here is a possible card for the climax scene:

INT-MANAGER'S OFFICE-DAY
Emma finds out she is the new manager.

The cards for the end of the movie might look like this:

EXT-GROCERY STORE PARKING LOT-DAY
Dave confronts Emma.
She admits she has the job.
Dave breaks up with Emma.

INT-EMMA'S HOUSE-NIGHT

Emma tells Sarah about promotion.

Sarah asks Emma to promise she won't work at a

grocery store her whole life.

INT-MANAGER'S OFFICE-DAY

Emma turns down the job.

EXT-PARKING LOT-DAY

Dave asks Emma if she wants to get back together.

She says no. Drives away in her car, which is packed with

all her stuff.

As she drives out of town, she honks at Elaine and the

new baker, who are passionately kissing.

Working backward

Some writers can envision the last scenes of the movie, the image they want to leave the viewer with, but cannot figure out how to get there. You can work backward from the picture in your head to figure out the scenes that need to come before. Concentrate on the picture in your mind, and take note of which characters appear. Every character should be in the scene for a specific reason. How did they come to be standing in the final picture you have in your mind? Do you need to add another scene to explain how they came to be there?

In the example above, Elaine and the new baker are standing outside the supermarket kissing as Emma drives away. If you wanted to give the audience more resolution to their story, you could add a scene between the climax and the ending that shows a little more of the relationship developing between them.

Twisting a conventional ending

You can end your screenplay many different ways, and almost all of them have been manipulated to no end. Often, trying to craft a surprise ending is what ruins the surprise ending. The audience can sense the over-manipulation when the writer plants surprise after surprise. One land mine, placed directly next to the previous land mine, is not going to surprise anyone. The movie *Knowing* tells the story of a young boy who experiences predictions after finding a strange sheet of numbers. The boy's father realizes the numbers are references to major world disasters and the amount of people that died due to them. As the movie draws to a close, the twists start to stack on top of each other. The boy reveals that the world will end and everyone will die. As they run for some kind of shelter, the father learns that aliens have come to take his son to a new planet to start all over. He lets go of his son, who boards the spaceship, and waits for the Earth's fiery end.

The amount of twists takes the movie from a stretch of the imagination to a little ridiculous. The audience can buy that one child might be affected by visions and that his father, spurred by his love and his scientific curiosity, buys into it. They can buy that ordinary people discover the date of the Armageddon, as several movies have depicted. They accept that aliens can exist.

What pushes it over the edge is the stacking of all of these ideas on top of each other. The audience only can suspend disbelief so far. Layering all these twists on the end of the movie, when there is little time to explain and rationalize them, leaves the audience feeling overwhelmed.

Let the surprise be more organic. After all, the surprise does not have to be surprising to everyone, only the character the audience is seeing the film's events through. Limiting the audience's view is an easy way to surprise them. If the audience only knows what that one character knows, the surprise should be more natural. This might make the writing more difficult, as you will have to limit what parts of the story the audience sees and resist putting them in a superior position. A classic example of this is *The Sixth Sense*, where the audience only gets the point of view of the protagonist. At the end, when he is caught by surprise, so are we.

Developing Themes in Your Screenplay

hile writing your screenplay, you have thought about the logline, the various story lines, and the dialogues of your screenplay. However, you might not yet have considered the motto of your screenplay or the message you want to send. You can write your first draft out completely and never think about the deeper meaning of your screenplay. But after the writing is completed, it is time for you to consider what overall message you want your story to send.

In the case of *Getting Out of Grossville*, your screenplay is a charming story about a woman who wants to overcome her circumstances and make a better life. You might think that there is no message; it is just a chick flick, a romantic comedy, some light entertainment that does not preach any message. But at the heart of every movie is a message, even in the screwiest of screwball comedies. So, for the grocery store comedy, the Emma we have described so far is not limited by the circumstances of her life; she is more limited by the ideas and expectations she and other people have for herself and the path she has set for herself so far. She always has focused on partying, relationships, and having a good time, but the screenplay tells the story of the time in her life when she tries to steer herself down another, more fulfilling path. During the course of her journey, she begins to apply herself to life and see what she can achieve. The moral of this story, depending on how it is written, could be many different things:

- Regardless of what people think, you can achieve your dreams. Emma could succeed in everything; she gets the job and the guy, who sweeps her off to a new glamorous life. Sarah also triumphs over her alcoholism. Elaine and the guy from the bakery live happily ever after.

- You are limited only by the restrictions you put on yourself. Emma triumphs over the obstacles to her getting what she really wants and realizes she was the only thing standing in her way. Elaine finally gets up the nerve to approach the bakery guy and discovers he is equally crazy about her, a fact she would have known long before if she had dared to approach him. Sarah gets over her stage fright and sings beautifully. She realizes her fear is the only thing stopping her from staying sober and succeeding.

- The relationships you develop make life full, not material success. Emma does not get the promotion, but during the course of her journey, she builds stronger relationships with her mom, Elaine, and her new love interest. She realizes that a fuller life in the same city is just as good as starting over in a new place. She also now has the confidence to look for a better job elsewhere and start a serious relationship with the guy.

Any of these could be your message depending on how you write it. The way you set up the story, the views you give the characters, the outcome of your hero's journey: These things contribute to the message. You can shape these aspects of the message to match the vision you have as a writer.

The central message the movie sends is the movie's theme. Every movie has a theme. It is not always obvious, and it is not something the characters preach to the audience. The audience understands the theme from various events that happen in the movie. Often, the events that transpire to the secondary characters echo the same overall theme.

The Greek Chorus

In ancient Greek plays, getting the theme of a movie across was made much easier by the chorus, who appeared on stage with the players and offered commentary and backstory for the audience. The cluster of people on stage might be gone, but the idea is still present in many different incarnations. Many modern works include some form of this: a character that breaks the fourth wall and speaks to the audience, offering criticism or opinion or a little clarification. Some examples:

- Statler and Waldorf (sometimes better known as the two cranky guys from the balcony) in the Muppet TV shows and movies would make sarcastic comments about whatever entertainment the Muppets offered.

- Timon and Pumbaa, sidekicks to Simba in the *Lion King*, offer the film's young audience an insight into something they might not otherwise pick up on. Timon explains to an oblivious Pumbaa how he can tell Simba and Nala are falling in love, just before they sing "Can you feel the love tonight?"

- The singer and guitar player in *There's Something About Mary* explain our main character, Ted, and his undying love for Mary, his high school crush at the film's opening. They appear at other points in the movie, reiterating how Mary is the only girl for Ted.

Fleshing Out a Theme

The theme of your screenplay might not come to you until after the writing is completed, and you look it over. Try to look at the overall story with fresh eyes and determine what message is coming across to the reader. Remember that the images, setting, and location of your scenes will have an impact on this as well. Try to envision the whole scene as you read to figure out what the viewer will take away from the scene.

You might prefer not to define a theme because you want to let the audience choose the message to take from the story. If this is the case, you still need to direct them toward the questions the screenplay is asking. If the theme of your screenplay is going to be "is cheating wrong?" instead of "cheating is wrong," make sure the thematic elements of your script are bringing this question to the forefront and offering different takes on the answer.

To identify the theme in your screenplay, answer the following questions:

- **What are your characters learning?** Over the course of the story, your characters should learn something. If no one in the movie learns anything, the story might seem unresolved and might pose a problem for the viewer.

- **What influence has the protagonist's journey had on other characters?** Some of your secondary characters might observe the action or comment on it from the outside. What is the message they learn from what happens to the hero? In *Goal! The Dream Begins*, Santiago Munez hopes to play soccer professionally. His father, a hardworking Mexican immigrant, discourages him from his dream and tries to get him to refocus his energy on a more practical goal. Near the movie's climax, when we see Santiago's father enter an American sports bar to watch a game Santiago plays in, we understand he is accepting the life that his son has chosen and that he is learning to be proud of his son.

- **How are their lives different than they were before the story began?** Maybe the change is small for a few of your characters. Their everyday lives might stay the same but now are punctuated with a glimmer of hope. This change, and how radical it is, speaks to the heart of your story. Is it a roll of the dice about how anyone's life can change on any day? Or is it about the payoff at the end of hard work and struggle?

- **How will they continue to change their lives?** As your characters go forward in their lives, where can the audience see them going? Are these places of optimism, or a realistic look at a bleak future?

- **What are the parallels between the protagonists' story and the stories that happen to the secondary characters?** There might be a natural similarity between the hero's journey and the events that happen to the other characters.

Classic themes with a twist

If you find yourself having trouble identifying the theme of your movie, think about the message at its core. Strip your movie's theme down to its central idea, and it likely will be a variation of an old idea. With a twist or a different angle on them, they become just different enough. Start with this core message and work your theme forward from there.

Love Conquers All

The most enduring of all themes is at the center of many big screen blockbusters. This seed of an idea can be turned into a comedy or a drama theme. Love conquers all — even the most mortifying of situations within the first weekend of meeting your future in-laws, as in *Meet The Parents*. Audiences love a good love story between a man and a woman, but they also enjoy a good family story about the love between parent and child or a family and their dog. Love for your dog conquers all, even his terrible behavior in *Marley and Me*. Even cynical audiences can enjoy a good love story, as long as it is well written and stands up to scrutiny.

Good Over Evil

Good triumphs over evil, and love proves more powerful than hate, in the last Harry Potter movie, *Harry Potter and the Deathly Hallows*. Other movies feature a group of people who band together to defeat an evil force, such as *Independence Day*. In *28 Days Later*, a small group fights against the rest of the population who have been turned into zombies.

David vs. Goliath

Everyone likes to root for an unlikely hero who defies the odds. Movies that go off this theme include whistle blower stories such as *Norma Rae*, in which one woman brings down a factory that pollutes a town, or *Erin Brockovich*, in which a down-on-her-luck single mom takes a job as a lawyer's secretary, then brings down a factory that pollutes a town. This theme also extends to underdog sports movies, such as *Cool Runnings*, a comedy about the first Jamaican bobsled team to compete at the Winter Olympics.

Wish Fulfillment, Be Careful What You Wish For

Movies about people who get their deepest desire, only to find it is not so great. This can take a divine twist, such as *Bruce Almighty* in which an ordinary guy gets to play God, to *Bedazzled* in which a man makes a deal with the devil to sell his soul for seven wishes. Age comedies, like *13 Going on 30, Big*, and *17 Again* take the approach of do not rush to be old or waste your life wanting to be young because you are where you are supposed to be in life. Movies in which one person experiences another's life, like *Freaky Friday* or *The Change Up*, show that the grass is not always greener on the other side. Even *Home Alone*, in which a young boy wished his family away for the holidays only to find he misses them, plays on the wish-fulfillment theme.

Highlighting the theme

Once you have identified the theme in your screenplay, you should highlight it. If you are not sure the theme is hitting home, consider adding a subplot that reinforces it more obviously or changing one of the existing subplots to highlight it.

Speaking the Theme

One of your characters might state the theme aloud. Without it being blatantly obvious, you can have one of your characters reinforce the theme or a similar thought. This is not to say you should beat the audience over the head with it. But if you can find a spot where the theme fits coming out of the hero's mouth, use it.

Let's say that after writing the movie about Emma, the theme of the movie turns out to be about following your dreams. The subplot about Sarah's alcoholism can be modified to help support this theme. Maybe Emma's mom always hoped to be a singer, but smoking and drinking ruined her voice and lung power. As Emma decides to follow her dream, her mom is inspired to do the same; she joins a band. In this way, the subplot now reinforces the "follow your dreams" theme. It is not the same as the main plot; Sarah's success is on a much smaller scale than Emma's. The subplot supports the main story but does not overshadow it.

If *Getting Out of Grossville* turned out to be less optimistic and Emma's story line is a less upbeat one, you could tweak the subplot to accommodate that. If the theme was "follow your dreams, but they might not be what you want when you get there," maybe Emma's mom has a good gig but finds that it does not take away her urge to drink. She realizes it is not the sadness over the loss of her singing career that drives her to want to drink, but the same old alcoholism she has fought all these years.

When the dominoes do not line up

While you want each character to arc, this does not mean a happy ending for each of them. Reinforcing the theme through subplots does not necessarily mean having every story end the same way. All of the characters do not have to have the same outcome as your protagonist. Maybe your hero will get the perfect ending but the secondary characters do not get what they want. Likewise, they do not have to fail just because the protagonist did. What matters is that the ending lines up with the overall theme.

If the theme is "cheaters never prosper," and the hero is a cheater, he will not get a happy ending. This does not mean other characters that have done the right thing should be denied a happy ending. But making good decisions will take you down a path similar to other people who have made good decisions. The same will hold true for your screenplay. Some characters will encounter good times as others fall on hard times.

Even in the darkest of times, there are rays of light in everyone's life, and you can show one of these moments to give the viewer hope for that character's future, even if the present we leave him or her in is less than ideal. If the story closes on a happy occasion like a wedding or family reunion, let this be the time to tie up some the strings regarding secondary characters and plotlines.

Symbolic Elements

Symbols can be used to highlight certain parts of the movie or the theme itself. They can punctuate what you are trying to say and strike home with the viewer.

A classic symbolic element is the girl in the red coat in *Schindler's List*. The most striking point of color in a black and white movie is a little girl who wears a red coat. She is seen walking down the street, where Schindler does not pay her much attention. The girl is later seen dead on a pile of bodies, waiting to be incinerated. The girl and more specifically her red coat have been interpreted as a symbol for Schindler's indifference to and subsequent realization of the war. She brought the death and horror of the war forward for him and personified the innocent Jews. The girl in the red coat is also seen as a symbol for the blind eye the rest of the world turned to the Holocaust as it was happening. If the theme of *Schindler's List* is that one life can make a difference, this girl in a red coat reinforces that by being one life that touches Schindler, who in turn touches many.

You can similarly use color and visual elements to emphasize certain parts of your script. Giving the audience a representation to drive your theme home can help them understand the important parts of your message. Your movie is not likely to be all black and white, but there are other ways to create a visually striking element. They can be the artifacts in your character's house, jewelry or personal effects, their car. All of these are everyday items. But they can be made different and attention grabbing. More than 25 years later, the leg lamp from *A Christmas Story* is still iconic and reproduced every Christmas as a novelty item. In the movie, the lamp was the source of arguments between Ralphie's father, who had won the lamp in a contest, and his mother, who thought it was tacky and vulgar. The lamp later broke, and whether it was truly an accident was the source of many more arguments.

Editing Your Screenplay

hen you go on a job interview, you might research the company, practice witty things to say, and study the field. But no matter how prepared you are on the inside, you still will take just as much care with the outside: choosing a special outfit, taking time to do your hair, and shining your shoes. Similarly, even if the message and story of your script are solid, the script still needs to be presented in its best possible form.

Aside from making sure the writing is dynamic and the dialogue sparkles, you also need to make sure your screenplay is up to professional standards. Attention to detail becomes important at this stage. The script should be formatted correctly and proofread carefully. Readers and agents are more likely to turn away from a script that is improperly formatted or dismiss the writer as an amateur if the script is riddled with typos and grammatical mistakes. Your script already will be in competition with many other scripts. Making sure it is free of errors can give you an advantage over other submissions that are not as diligent.

In addition to running a computer spell-checker, proofread it yourself because the computer cannot detect contextual errors. Also, check to make sure the names of characters and places are consistent throughout. You also can use this time to check any facts that might be in the script. If one of the characters gives the population of the United States, make sure the figure they give is current. This preparation shows a level of commitment and that you take the craft seriously. If you have taken the time to do your research and learn the way professional scripts are submitted, they will accept you as a professional. Even if the writing of your script is truly amazing, no one is going to notice if the spelling and grammar are poor.

Formatting Your Screenplay

A completed screenplay should have a cover page, with the name of your screenplay, followed by "a screenplay by" the name of the author(s). In the bottom right hand corner, list the contact details for yourself, or if you have representation, you can list your representation's contact details in that corner.

You do not need to add a date to the title page or to any portion of the script. A date can add an unwanted air of staleness. There is nothing wrong with a script you wrote last year; however, in seeing the date on the page, the readers might get the impression your script is no good because no one has bought it yet. They might assume you have only sent it to them after others have turned it down, or as a last-ditch effort. Likewise, do not number your draft; it is not necessary and only serves to clutter your title page. You might feel proud your first draft is perfect, but the reader might think you have not done any work to make the script better. Conversely, if you send the sixth draft, they might think it must be a bad script if it required so much tinkering. Number the pages, but do not number the scenes. If you script is purchased, the director and studio might choose to reorder them.

The accepted font for screenplays is Courier or Courier New, 12 point. All professional screenwriters use this font, as one page typed in it has been found to translate perfectly to one minute of screen time. Using another font or cheating by using a different font size will mark you as an amateur. The experienced reader will be able to identify this kind of page manipulation just by looking at it. Leave the right margin on the default setting, and set the left margin at 1.5 inches. The dialogue should be centered, with the character's name above the lines he or she speaks, like this.

JOHN
I made this for you.

Scene descriptions are left aligned and single-spaced.

John stands in front of Nicole. He carries a large shoulder bag and a bouquet of roses. Roger stands just behind him.

Characters names are capitalized only as they first appear and over a line of dialogue that they will speak.

ROGER PETERSON, 44, is a blond All American, built like a linebacker but smart as a whip.

In a novel, the author has the choice of present or past tense. But in film, when everything is happening now, the script has to be in present tense. The scene descriptions and actions should be kept as concise and to the point as you can.

If you interrupt a character's speech with an action, you can indicate it in parentheses, as long as the same character is doing the action.

JOHN
I made this for you.

(reaches into his bag)

Here.

If someone else is doing the action, indicate this from the left-hand side, as you would scene description.

JOHN
I made this for you.

Roger hands him the box.

JOHN
(continued)

Here.

In the movie business, the heading line is also known as a slug line. This is the line discussed back in Chapter 7. It abbreviates the camera location of exterior or interior, the location of the scene, and the time the scene is taking place. The slug line should be written in all caps.

Movie Writing Software

For a beginning screenwriter, screenwriting software might seem like an unnecessary expense because you can successfully build scripts in Microsoft® Word. However, constantly having to switch your formatting every time you go from dialogue to slug line and back again is exhausting and wastes time that you could be writing. Setting margins, styles, and formatting in each section requires you to know a little about Word. If you only have a limited time every day to write, being more efficient during that time could make you a lot more productive overall.

As an alternative to Word, you could invest in a program available for screenwriters. Final Draft is arguably the best known in the United States and is widely used. Movie Magic Screenwriter is Final Draft's biggest competitor, and it offers similar functions. Both programs feature templates for movie scripts, as well as a function with which the computer can read the script aloud to you. For writers who work in teams, both programs offers file sharing via real time Internet. New for 2012, Adobe® Creative Suite® introduced Story, a program designed for writing scripts. Projects written in Story can be integrated with projects created in Adobe Premiere®.

Seeking Feedback

Finishing a screenplay is a monumental achievement. You have a right to feel proud of what you have done. Regardless of what happens after this moment, you have proven your discipline and creativity. However, if you do hope to sell the script, this is simply a break. More work is still to be done.

Once your script is truly finished, each word perfect and with your stamp of approval on each page, it is time to put it away.

Take a break from the project for about two weeks, if you can stay away from it for that long; you might have ideas for how to make the screenplay better during this time. Make a note of them, but then put them away until the break is over.

After you bring it out and read it over, you might have more ideas on how to improve it. One you have made all the adjustments you can think of, now is the time to see what others think of it. Seeking feedback from a fresh pair of eyes is a way to get helpful suggestions on what is not working and how to fix it. Additional readers also might help decide everything is working fine. You might find it hard to know when to stop tinkering with the script. If the feedback that comes back is related to small things, or mostly positive, it might be time to stop making changes and accept that the writing stage is over.

Print a full script for your first readers, and ask them to read the whole thing before offering any opinions. Do not badger them or ask them for updates as they review the script. Allow them enough time to finish and fully digest the script.

Opening yourself up to feedback

It can be hard to open yourself to criticism, especially on a screenplay you have worked so hard on. Even showing your work to family and close friends can be hard, as they are the closest to you, and you might want their approval more than anyone else's. The people you trust are doubtlessly people you love and value, but they are far from perfect. They might not know how to offer feedback without being overly critical or hurtful. Alternately, they could be scared to tell you the whole truth about what they think.

You might want to give copies of the script to your mom, siblings, and best friends, which is great. But consider how they will react to your script. When you choose people to seek feedback from, try to select people who will give you the kind of criticism you can handle. If you prefer direct, to-the-point comments and are not scared of honest criticism, then solicit feedback from people who are more honest. If you prefer a softer approach, try a friend you know to be more tactful. Perhaps you have a friend or family member who has experience as a teacher, professor, counselor or who works in a supervisor position. He or she might have training in how to offer feedback in a positive manner. If you are still nervous about receiving feedback, try creating a feedback sheet that asks questions directly related to the screenplay and what you feel needs work. This can save you from getting overly negative responses. As time goes on and you get more accustomed to receiving feedback, you will learn that it is not anything to dread. The people you solicit feedback from are trying to provide you with helpful information to make your screenplay better.

Remember in any group of people, there will be outliers. If you give your script to a group of ten people, be prepared for mixed results. Two may gush about how great it is; two might be overly harsh. The rest might fall in the middle somewhere. When receiving feedback, it is important to look past the comments you do not like to see the value in them. Always remember that these people are trying to help you, so be grateful to them for their time and help.

Online feedback

Some sites online allow you to post your script and solicit feedback from other writers. Trigger Street Labs (**http://labs.trigger-street.com**) is a social community for aspiring writers and filmmakers looking to get feedback and exposure for their work.

Professional feedback

Sending your script out for feedback from a professional is a big decision. Although some writers feel that anyone charging money for feedback is a scam artist, others feel it is money well spent. When you send your screenplay for evaluation, the person reviews your script and provides feedback and notes. This service also is called coverage. Coverage is also the term for the report a professional reader at a studio would prepare on a newly submitted script. This report is what the agent reviews first before attempting to undertake reading the whole script. The reader will give the script a recommendation: pass, meaning a rejection, or consider, meaning the script is worth a look. Traditionally, coverage is a synopsis of the movie's plot, as well as an opinion on several aspects of the script. The dialogue, character development, and plot structure all are given a rating.

If you hire a script consultant, expect to pay per page to receive a commentary on your script. The consultant might suggest changes that can be made to the overall project as well as more specific ideas for portions of the script that particularly need work. You can Google the reputation of any decent script consultant. He or she should be able to offer some references that you can ask about their experiences.

Rewriting Your Script

After getting the feedback on your script and working on it, you might find that you need to undertake a rewrite. A rewrite can be a total new start, known as a Page One rewrite, or it simply can be adjustments to a portion of the script. If you did not write from your story cards, you might find yourself going back and rewriting to add in exposition or setups you forgot.

After finally finishing the first draft, a rewrite might be the last thing you want to deal with. Rewriting your script, or even a portion of it, can be scary. After all, losing the precious page count you have is not something any writer wants to face, especially if the minutes you take to write your script are difficult to come by. But if the script is not working perfectly, you owe it to yourself to try something new, something creatively unrestricted. Do not be afraid to try it again. You always can try rewriting a small portion instead of undertaking a Page One rewrite unless you find the complete rewrite necessary.

When rewriting, it might be best to lay out the new direction you hope to take on story cards first. You can pin these cards on top of the original cards they replace. You can try them in different configurations with the existing cards to see if the full rewrite is necessary or if changing a scene or two might solve the problems you have.

If you only rewrite a portion of the script, make sure that portion still fits into the framework of the story and the continuity is still there. Everything that needs to happen is still there. Everything still makes sense. After creating the new section, read it over again along with the sections just before and after it.

If you have undertaken a rewrite because all the necessary parts of your script are there but the script is just not interesting, look at each scene to see where it is losing steam. Start with the most important scenes: the opening, ending, climax, midpoint, and plot points. If these scenes are not popping off the page, consider why. Listen to your instincts concerning what is wrong. Look at the page to see if the writing is out of balance. Maybe you know what section is not working but you are not sure why. Or worse, you know what is wrong but you cannot figure out how to fix it. If you find yourself overwhelmed, look at each scene individually. Just like in the original writing process, it is easier to tackle this in small increments than as a large block. As you read and analyze each scene, assess whether this scene is contributing to the hero's journey. Every scene has to be telling the audience something about the journey, the motivations behind it, and the aspirations that fuel it.

Read the script all the way through once without stopping to analyze. Then read again, this time taking the time to make notes on each scene and what needs work. If you have a printed version of your script, make notes by hand on this copy. If you are reading on the computer, the program you created the document in likely has a way to add notes to the screenplay directly next to the portion of script it refers to. In Microsoft Word, this is the comments feature, found under the Review tab. You also can track the changes you make to the document with the Track Changes feature, also found under the Review tab. This way, you can hold on to the parts you cut in the same document. Then, you can go through scene by scene and see what needs to be done to address the issues.

Try to categorize the problem in each scene. Is the problem the content, that not enough is happening? Or is the style of writing that is too dense?

If you feel that not enough is happening over the course of your story, you can try a few things:

- Look at condensing the events into a shorter script. Make things happen faster. Go back to your first ten pages and see if you can cut out anything. Have the first incident, the one that sets your journey in motion, happen faster. Do not leave the audience any time up front to be bored. Introduce only the things that need to be there: the high points of the scene, the parts they need to know, the characters they will meet. Do not waste any time or scenes on any extra introductions. Cut down to the simplest form of the story, and see if it still holds your interest.

- Add more complications. The hero should have to work hard to get what he or she wants. If your second act is lagging or feels long, you might need to make the protagonist's journey even harder. Remember, the audience will not feel satisfied that the hero has done enough to get what he or she really wants if he or she does not have to fight for it.

- Is there enough conflict in the scene? Each scene should have a conflict, and if the scene falls flat, it might be because the conflict needs tweaking. Is the conflict something of consequence? If the characters are fighting over something small, maybe the scene does not have enough at stake or maybe the conflict is not clear enough. Go back to the index card you created for this scene and look at the points listed on it. These are the essential points. Are they coming through in the finished scene? Is each character's motivation in the conflict clear? Why do the characters want what they want, and is it coming across to the audience?

- Add interest to the script. Add more interesting things to the scene. If the scenes are feeling static, move them to a different location that has not been seen yet in the script. Take your characters to a location they are not used to, where they would not normally go, and see what that brings out of them. You do not have to add everything to every scene; just adding some symbolism to a scene can make it more interesting. You can use a scene that does not have much action to create tension within the script.

If the writing is too dense, try to see if there is anything you can show instead of tell. Cut whatever you can this way. Ask yourself in each scene:

- Can you show the viewer what this location is? Instead of wasting words explaining where the characters are and why, see if you can incorporate a sign, flyer, or billboard telling the audience where they are. Sometimes the place itself is recognizable enough without the audience being specifically told what it is. You do not need to tell them "This is the school." Instead, put the protagonist in the hallway outside a classroom with children's artwork all over the walls, and have the protagonist's child run past toward the door. The message is sent in about ten seconds and is much more interesting than having the protagonist on his or her cell phone outside the school saying, "I have to call you back. I'm at my kid's school."

- If your movie is a comedy, how can you add physical comedy to the scene? Instead of telling all the jokes, show some. Physical comedy does not have to be slapstick. It can be one person dressed wrongly for a fancy occasion. It can be one character's pain (if played right). It can be the straight face of one character as something intensely funny is happening that he or she absolutely cannot laugh at. Physical jokes do not have to be gross or cheap. They can come from the funny, awkward moments of life.

- Hack away the unnecessary words. Remember, in a screenplay, there is no room for prose and description. A screenplay conveys a series of events and a series of actions.

- Trust the actors. You might think the actors need words to express how your characters are feeling. If they are talented actors, they can convey their characters' emotions through their craft. You do not have to overwrite. For example:

Jesse enters the kitchen confidently.

JESSE
Honey, I'm home!

Jesse walks through the kitchen, turning his head from left to right, looking around each doorway to see if she is hiding. Shaking his head, he walks up to the dining table and reads the note on it.

JESSE

No! No!

He shakes his head and finally lays it between his hands on the table, tears running down his face.

Instead of the example above, this simpler version allows room for some creative interpretation:

Jesse enters the kitchen smiling.

JESSE

Honey, I'm home!

Jesse looks around the kitchen area, then walks to the dining table and reads the note on it.

JESSE

No! No!

He begins to cry.

The actor playing Jesse will want to make some choices of his own. Part of the joy of an actor's job is taking the material and making it his or her own. A good screenwriter knows actors will want to make their own choices about how and why the characters do the things they do.

Marketing Your Screenplay

Inside the Hollywood system, a writer writes the script, an agent sells the script, publicists publicize it and create a buzz around it, and producers put up the money to get it made. You are about to undertake many of these jobs at once. You are the only one who knows how good your story is, how much it merits being sold and being made into a feature on the big screen. Now it is your turn to convince other people. Your screenplay is the underdog, fighting for a chance to see light. You will have to find someone to champion the film, someone who loves it almost as much as you do.

The truth is that getting your screenplay sold is the hardest part of the journey so far. Getting an agent to look at your screenplay is incredibly difficult for a first-time writer, especially if you do not have any contacts in the industry. The competition is tough, with many writers knocking on all the doors. Being persistent and handling rejection well is an important part of this process. The lead time between when you start trying and when you manage to sell the script can be long. How many rejections do you think you can handle before wanting to give up? Take that number and double it. Now you are ready to begin selling your script.

Copyrighting Your Work

Before you can really start the work of searching for an agent and trying to sell your script, you need to take a few steps to protect yourself. The script that now sits in front of you is considered your intellectual property. It is something tangible you created that you now own and have exclusive rights to. The purpose of copyrighting your work is to protect your intellectual property and registering the date you finished your screenplay. Under the law, your work belongs to you from the minute you create it. However, if you should ever need to prove that time in court, the copyright is what the law recognizes.

The copyright grants you and only you the rights to this work, which includes making copies of the work, derivative works, and performing the work. No one can use your screenplay as a basis for another work, perform your work, or distribute copies of your work without getting your permission and compensating you. They also cannot create a derivative work, or a work that borrows from the characters or major points of your work so heavily that it is not considered an original. It is not likely you will run into any problems, but a copyright is a fairly easy and affordable way to protect yourself.

The Poor Man's Copyright

Many writers have heard about the poor man's copyright, the process of mailing a copy of the script to yourself and keeping the sealed envelope with the postmark as proof of the script's date of completion. The U.S. Copyright Office cautions against this, as the law does not recognize it. However, for the price of a few dollars, it could be helpful in the unlikely case of a lawsuit or copyright dispute, for example, if you felt someone stole or copied your idea in the time between when you write it and the time you submit it for a copyright. If you like to have insurance, spend a few dollars and keep the envelope in a drawer, just in case.

Copyrights through the U.S. Copyright Office

Copyrighting your work is the process of registering your intellectual property with the U.S. Copyright Office. The copyright protects your work from the moment you created it, but because that can be hard to prove, the date the copyright office grants your application is the official date. You will get a certificate of registration from them in the mail that shows this date. The copyright protection lasts 70 years after your death.

The process of copyrighting is fairly simple and can be done a few different ways. You can apply for a copyright online at the U.S. Copyright Office website, **www.copyright.gov**. This carries a lower fee and has a faster processing time. The online method allows you to track the progress of your submission. The processing time for a copyright application can be long, and if you apply by mail, you will not be able see how your application is progressing. To process your application this way, complete the online form, pay the $35 fee, and upload a copy of your work.

If you choose to mail your forms, the copyright office recommends you print and use their form CO, which contains a barcode the office can use to scan the form. The copyright application then is processed much faster than if you complete your forms by hand. This form can be printed from their website and mailed in with your script and the $50 filing fee. If you prefer, you can fill in the forms by hand and mail it in the old-fashioned way. The processing time for this type of submission can be four to five months.

Registering your script with the WGA

The WGA or Writers Guild of America also offers you the ability to register your script. The guild itself is split into two sections, East and West, with offices in Los Angeles and New York serving writers. To join the WGA, you need to do work for a company the Guild recognizes. By working for a recognized company, you earn units with the guild based on the amount of work you do. After you have a certain amount of units, you can join as an associate member, and once you gain some more, you become a current member.

You do not need to be a member of the WGA to register your script; this is a separate service the WGA provides. Once registered with the WGA, you are offered five years of protection, which is similar to but does not replace a copyright. You also can register treatments, outlines for ideas, and drafts with the WGA. To register your script, pay the registration fee, and upload the document to the WGA website (**www.wga.org** or **www.wgaeast. org**). The fee to register with the WGA is $20 for non-members. The work then is considered deposited with the WGA. Think of it as in safekeeping, locked away in a room somewhere. If you submit a hard copy of your work, it literally is deposited somewhere under lock and key, and only the registered writer can request copies of it or access it.

Once your script is protected under the law, you can start preparing to sell your script.

Researching the Market

The next part of your work involves a different kind of research and writing. Research agents, industry contacts, contests, and other possible existing contacts you might be able use to get your script submitted. This is much less creative work, but no less worthwhile than the writing of the actual scripts. You could write the best script in the world, but if you do not put the same effort into the sales pitch, it might never become known. To give your script the best chance of selling, you need to target the right agents, those interested in the kind of screenplay you have written. If you are going to enter contests to get noticed, you need to enter those you have a chance of winning or that can benefit you in some way. Even though the fee to enter most contests is minimal, you do not want to waste even a small amount of money.

Knowing the kind of market you are attempting to sell your work in can only benefit you. By familiarizing yourself with the kinds of deals that have been made recently and the climate in Hollywood, you can make your pitch more effective.

The market for your script can vary based on many factors:

- **Recent films:** As stated above, it can take a long time to go from inception to having a script ready to go. So you might have a great unique idea for a script, and just as you have finished it, you discover that another movie almost identical to yours is about to be released by a major studio. Does this mean you cannot sell your script? Not necessarily, but it might make the process more involved. Every movie has been made before, so that alone should not stop you from trying to sell your script. But you might need to research the similar movie and highlight the way your script is different from the one that has already come out.

- **Recent hits:** No one sees movies with women in the lead roles. Minority movies sell half as often because they produce less of those every year. We have all heard these conventions, and yet they do not stand up to the test of time. Every year new movies defy the old wisdom and prove the rules are not true. If your movie has a woman as the star, research the recent box office to see what films in the same vein have sold recently. You can use this information to illustrate how marketable movies similar to yours are.

- **Recent sales:** Would you pitch your own space odyssey the week after a well-established sci-fi screenwriter sold one to the same studio? Not such a great idea. However, if one studio has purchased a space odyssey, another studio might be looking for a similar movie to compete with it. Or they already might have one in production. Publications like *Variety* and *The Hollywood Reporter* detail the latest Hollywood deals and are available in print or online. By keeping up with the latest deals in Hollywood, you can get a hold on what Hollywood is buying. This can help you understand the climate of the current market.

- **Recent technology:** If you aspire to be a filmmaker as well as a writer, you do not need to sell your script. You can make it happen yourself. Computer animation is easier to use and, in the case of some programs, cheaper to obtain than ever before. You can recruit local actors, camera operators, and editors to help with the project. If you live near a school that offers a film major or curriculum, you might be able to get together with a student and have the movie made as a student film.

The Sale Process

The process of selling your script can take several different paths, but most likely, you will start with the conventional path and try to interest an agent in representing your script. The agent then will try to sell your script to a studio. You also can try to sell the script directly to a studio using a lawyer or manager as your way in. Screenwriting contests also abound; some of them offer cash prizes only, others offer access to people in the industry and exposure.

To sell your screenplay, you will create new documents, treatments, and outlines and work up a sales pitch. You will be working on query letters and treatments to pitch your script to people in the industry. This is where the editing skills you honed on the screenplay come in handy.

Selling your script is really selling yourself: your talent as a writer, your proofreading skills, and the genius idea that has driven you this far. Get ready to talk more about yourself and your work than you ever have. If you are a shy person, now is the time to put that aside. Start by telling family and friends your idea. Practice telling them about your script, emphasizing the interesting parts and streamlining your synopsis.

The agent

Finding an agent to champion your work gives you a distinct advantage. Agents have connections to get your script into the hands of people who have the power to buy it and get it made. Most major Hollywood studios will not look at unsolicited manuscripts. Others will accept them and place them on a slush pile for a reader to look at sometime down the line. Having an agent that can place the script directly in the hands of someone who is interested gives you a much better chance of making a sale.

Seeking an agent can be a long process, and requires you to be tenacious. You might have to wait a long time to hear back from the agents you solicit because they also might have a slush pile, though it is doubtlessly smaller than the one at the studio. Familiarize yourself with the process so you can make sure everything is done the right way and your submission is not sent back for a trivial reason. In addition to looking at the content of your work, the agent also is going to look at the cover letter to see how professionally you communicate. He or she will look at the formatting of the script to see if it is up to industry standards. An agent does not want to be embarrassed by sending out a script with spelling or formatting errors in it. It reflects badly on you and his or her agency.

If you have been following the latest Hollywood news and deals, you already might be familiar with the names of some of Hollywood's best agents. You can research lesser-known agents online or in print. The WGA offers a full list of agents on their website (**www.wga.org/agency/agencylist.aspx**), which you do not have to a be a member to access. There are also directories in print, such as the *2012 Guide to Literary Agents* by Chuck Sambuchino, an editor for Writer's Digest Books.

After compiling a list of agencies, research each one to see their submission process. Some agents now accept submissions and queries online, while others prefer regular mail. Most agencies do not accept unsolicited manuscripts. The amount of material this would add up to would just be overwhelming for them if every new screenwriter sent them a hundred pages. This is a good thing for you because it cuts out the cost of copying and mailing your whole script multiple times. You might think sending the whole script cannot hurt because once they open it and read the first few pages they will be so sucked in they will read the rest. But they likely will recycle or toss it without even opening it. To get them to read the script, you have to be invited to send it to them. So how can you get an agent interested in your script? This is where the first of your new documents, your query letter, comes in.

The query letter

Your query letter is a one-page representation of your screenplay. No matter how much you feel you have to say or explain about your story, do not be tempted to extend it beyond a page. This is where the editing skills you have improved while working on your script can come back into play.

The letter needs to pique the agent's interest enough to make him or her want to request the whole script and read it. It also needs to tell them a little about you, your credentials, and your qualifications. If you have any connection to this agent — say a friend has worked with him or her, you met him or her at a networking event, or you went to school together a long time ago — you can bring that up in the letter. You also can mention your accomplishments, such as any published writings or awards you might have won for writing. If your screenplay is about firefighters and you have 20 years experience in the field, you would mention this here.

It might seem like a lot of information to stuff onto one page, but you do not want the letter to be too dense. Leaving some white space makes the letter look more appealing to the eye. It is important to show here that you can be concise and stick to the accepted format of a query letter. Again, this illustrates your professionalism and how knowledgeable you are about the industry.

Do not rush this part of the process, as it is just as important as the writing of your script. These days, most of our communication is electronic and sent as quickly as possible, with spelling mistakes and grammatical errors abundant. And it is true that writing the average letter might take you a few minutes, or an hour at the most. But this letter is worth looking at multiple times to make sure it is clear and concise. Take your time, and make sure the cover letter tells the story of your script in an interesting way. If you forget to mention something in an email, you easily can send another. However, this query letter is your one shot to make a good impression on an agent. If it is not done well, he or she might never be willing to look at your full script.

Here is an example of a cover letter, written to solicit an agent for *Getting Out of Grossville*

Date

Bob Johnson
Johnson Agency
101 Johnson Road
Hollywood CA 90028

Dear Mr. Johnson,

My new script, *Getting Out of Grossville* is about Emma, a young woman tired of her life as a grocery store cashier, who decides to take her chance to change her fate. To escape her alcoholic mother and small town, she needs to do whatever it takes to get a manager job at the grocery store. The only thing standing between her and the extra income she needs to make her dream come true is the other candidate for the job — Emma's new boyfriend and possible love of her life. *Getting Out of Grossville* is a coming-of-age story about finding love, but ultimately, finding yourself.

The script was chosen as Best New Script in the True North Screenplay Contest. My short fiction has also won numerous awards.

The complete script is ready and available for your review. I can be reached by phone at (123) 456-7890, email at grocerystoremovie@mail.com, or by using the enclosed self-addressed, stamped envelope.

Sincerely,

Author's name

Cover Letter Tips

If you have experience writing cover letters for business or for your resume when soliciting jobs, some of the same guidelines apply:

- Address the letter to one specific agent instead of "to whom it may concern" or "sir or madam." This shows you took the time to research the business and what each agent specializes in.

- Check your spelling carefully, and check your grammar and punctuation. Using spell-check is not thorough enough. For example, a proper name such as Isabella will not be marked as wrong in a standard Microsoft Word spell-check. But alternate spellings like Izabella, Issabella, or the nickname Izzy will be marked misspelled. If you use one of these as a character name, you will have to manually check that each instance is spelled correctly and spelled the same way. You also could add your character's name into your spell-checker to make sure it alerts you when it is spelled incorrectly. This holds true for words as well as names. Another example: If you are trying to type the word "good" but accidentally type "food," The spell check will not see this as incorrect. Be sure to go over your letter carefully, line by line, to make sure it is as perfect as possible.

- Check that you are spelling the agent's name correctly. Agent Isabella Johnson might spell her name Izzabella Jonson.

- Use business English. Even if the movie is aimed at teens and written in slang, the agent will see how skilled you are at writing in that style when they read the screenplay. Now is the time to showcase yourself as a professional.

Sending the query letters

Querying can be a disheartening process. Some screenwriters get discouraged at this point. You can send your query letters to multiple agents at the same time because the response time on queries is long. But the numbers might surprise you; if you send out a hundred queries, you might only see ten responses, if that. For the majority of the queries you send out, you will get no response. Other agents might respond with form letters saying the work is not for them or that they do not accept unsolicited material. If they are really emphatic about not accepting unsolicited queries, they might return your query without opening it.

However, if you persevere, you might get the ideal response: an agent who wants to see your whole script. You then can draft a new cover letter, thanking the agent for his or her interest. It is also good to work in a mention of the fact that the agent requested the whole script. That way you have no chance of your script being mistaken for an unsolicited manuscript and getting pushed to the side. Enclose a self-addressed stamped envelope for return correspondence.

Here is a sample cover letter to send with your requested script:

May 6, 2012

Bob Johnson
Johnson Agency
101 Johnson Road
Hollywood CA 90028

Dear Mr. Johnson,

Thank you so much for your prompt response regarding my script, *Getting Out of Grossville*. I am enclosing the entire, script, as you requested in your correspondence on May 4, 2012.

As a reminder, this script is the personal journey of Emma, a young woman tired of her life as a grocery store cashier, who decides to take her chance to change her fate. To escape her alcoholic mother and small town, she needs to do whatever it takes to get a manager job at the grocery store. The script was chosen as Best New Script in the True North Screenplay Contest. My short fiction has also won numerous awards.

If you have any other questions or concerns, I can be reached by phone at (123) 456-7890, email at grocerystoremovie@ mail.com, or by using the enclosed self-addressed stamped envelope. I look forward to hearing from you soon.

Sincerely,

Author's name

Entering contests

Screenwriting contests are a controversial topic. Most screenwriting contests charge an entry fee, usually not more than $40 to $50, which is fairly affordable. However, some writers object not to the amount of the fee, but the idea of spending any money on something that might not pay off. At the heart of this argument is the use of readers. Just like a studio, the contest might use readers to get through the large amount of submissions and whittle them down. The reader might not know anything about screenwriting and is not going to offer you any feedback. Some writers feel the money is better spent on coverage from a professional with actual screenwriting credits. Others say the money is better spent on submission materials, your bills, and gummy bears, anything but a screenwriting contest.

Another point against screenwriting contests is that they can be demoralizing. You pay your money, send in your script, and never hear a thing back. Your chances of winning can be slim if it is a nationally or internationally known contest. Then again, sending your screenplay out to agents, hoping a reader will grab it off the stack, like it, and present it to the agent, is also a risky venture with slim chances for success. So, which is better? It is up to you, how much you believe in your script, and the path you decide is right for you. If you have a thick skin and the added rejection of not winning contests will not faze you, screenwriting contests can open doors for you and give you added credentials when promoting your script to agents if you do win anything in the contests.

When choosing screenwriting contests, research them carefully to see if you can discern who will be reading your script. Some contests, such as The Scriptapalooza Screenplay Contest, do not use readers to review submissions. Instead, agents, managers, and producers read all scripts themselves. Also, even if your script does not win any awards, if the analysts decide other professionals should read the script, he or she will send your script (with your permission) to a select list of agents. When considering a contest, find out the success of past winners. Take some time to Google the winners of recent years and see if they have found representation, made any deals since winning the contest, or sold the script that won.

Contest: The Scriptapalooza Screenplay Contest

The Scriptapalooza Screenplay Contest is one of the best known contests for aspiring screenwriters. Launched in 1998, Scriptapalooza focuses on offering screenwriters exposure and access to readers who can option the script. By submitting their script, screenwriters are afforded a chance for producers and agents to look over their work. If named as a semifinalist, screenwriters also are represented and promoted by the Scriptapalooza people for a year. In addition to the $10,000 prize, the access to people in Hollywood is valuable for an aspiring screenwriter. Scriptapalooza promises actual managers, agents, and producers read through the scripts submitted to them instead of using readers.

Alternate Ways to Get A Movie Made

ost screenwriters would like to see their movie made but would also like to make some money while doing it, not to mention the fame and success that can come with a Hollywood sale. For those reasons, many screenwriters try to break into the Hollywood system. The way outlined in the previous chapter is the way that has proven most successful, though it can take a long time and a lot of rejections to break through.

If you are tired of sending query after query, try these alternate ways of getting your script noticed. Another way some writers are able to get their scripts looked at by someone in the Hollywood system is by using the contacts they already have. Networking and keeping in touch with the contacts you have can open doors for you.

Networking

Just as you have taken up screenwriting, you may have friends, family members, neighbors, community members, church members, or coworkers who dabble in some aspect of film. If they cannot personally help you, they might know someone who can.

Having someone refer or introduce you to a friend does not have to be awkward or difficult for you. Being prepared and professional in your approach helps other people take you seriously and feel confident about introducing you to their contacts. It is also good to be reachable in many ways. Some people find it easier to fit emails into their schedule, while others would rather talk on the phone or meet for coffee. For less than $100, you can have business cards made and set up your own domain name for your website. This allows you to get the word out about yourself online and to people you meet in person.

Online networking

With the invention of the Internet, finding like-minded people is easier than ever. As a screenwriter, you can use this ease of access to your advantage. Sites such as Linkedin® make it easy to keep track of your potential contacts. Linkedin is a professional networking site similar to social networking sites like Facebook or MySpace. However, instead of being used only as a resource for finding your friends, Linkedin connects you to professional contacts. Once you connect to the people you know, you can see if any of them can connect you to someone who can help with your script. If you are intimated or nervous about asking for help, this is one way to cut down the number of inquiries you have to make. Instead of approaching every friend you have, you only will have to approach two or three you know to have a useful connection.

Just because Facebook and MySpace are not known for being professional sites does not mean they cannot be useful. Once you get your website set up, use these sites for their marketing potential. Send your website out to all your friends for exposure. The more people you get excited about your screenplay, the better your chance of it reaching someone who can turn it into a movie.

Sites also exist to help you promote a completed screenplay. A website mentioned earlier in the book, Trigger Street Labs (**http://labs.triggerstreet.com**) defines itself as a platform for aspiring filmmakers and writers to gain exposure and attention for their scripts and projects. Site members begin by critiquing and reviewing scripts submitted by other users. They receive credits for doing this, and once they have enough credit, they can post their own work to the site for review. This helps you receive constructive criticism, but it also helps you network with other writers and aspiring filmmakers. It lets you act as a reader, in a sense, theoretically leading to the best scripts being featured and spotlighted on the site. Trigger Street is an actual production company founded by actor Kevin Spacey, and it sponsors contests and festivals promoted through the site.

Setting up your own website

Choose a domain name that is straightforward and easy to re-member. Your first and last name is a good option, unless you have a name that is easily misspelled, difficult to remember, or so common that someone has taken it already. You also can choose a domain name relevant to your new career, such as www.jerry-thescreenwriter.com.

If your screenplay has a title you are set on, you could create a domain name with that title instead, such as www.gettingoutof-grossville.com. However, if you choose the name of your current project, you might have to create new or separate sites for every project, instead of promoting yourself as a whole. Maybe that is the approach you would like to take, but you might want to tie them together somehow, maybe through a blog that focuses more on you.

If you can afford to have a professional design a site for you, it might be worth doing so. Web design has its own principles, and having a well-designed, organized website is to your advantage. It looks more professional and makes a better impression on a viewer. In some cases, novice mistakes you make trying to design your own site make the content hard to read or find, and people turn away from the site. If you cannot afford professional design, many hosting providers offer templates you can use to make a generic but perfectly useful site. A screenwriter's website to look at for inspiration is **www.johnaugust.com**. The site promotes screenwriter John August, but also offers news about screenwriting, information about his projects, and other information in a streamlined, clean-looking site.

Once your website or blog is set up, keep it updated. This will keep readers coming back for more and will keep it at the tops of keyword searches on the Internet. Also, make sure all your business cards feature this website and that it is prominently displayed on all your social networking sites, such as Linkedin, Facebook, and MySpace.

If the thing that matters most to you is seeing your story as a movie, not necessarily a Hollywood blockbuster, you can try a few other things. You can try to get the film made as an independent film or team with film students to produce the movie as a student film. The remainder of this chapter will cover these uncommon options.

Independent Films

Independent film is a broad term, used to describe any movie that has been produced without the financing or support of the studio system. Independent filmmaking traces its roots back to the days when filmmakers were restricted by a code and studio financing. Those who wanted to express themselves or make a film about a risqué or less-than-wholesome subject had to do so outside of the studios, which would not finance those movies. Those who could not find a champion at the studio for their movies also had to find another way. Filmmakers who wanted to tell stories that had ambiguous endings went this way, as did horror and science fiction directors who wanted to gross audiences out with gore.

These days, independent films do not necessarily have to be about a controversial topic. This type of film is produced more easily than ever due to the lower cost and easy accessibility of filmmaking equipment. Studios are more interested in purchasing these films and distributing them. Independent films that have won festivals or gotten press attention can take off and become a hit. They usually carry smaller costs, so they are easier for the studio to purchase cheaply and make a profit on.

Independent vs. art house

Many people confuse independent films with art house films. Art house films tend to be aimed at a specific market. Directors or writers of art house films might do away with typical structure or convention in order to make an artistic statement or deliver a message. Independents can be traditional and structured in the same way as Hollywood blockbusters. *My Big Fat Greek Wedding*, which was made as an independent film, went on to be one of the top grossing romantic comedies of all time. You may think you have never seen an independent film, but some have gotten distribution deals, become sleeper hits, and then have become household names. Some more examples:

- *The Blair Witch Project*
- *The Artist*
- *Midnight In Paris*
- *Little Miss Sunshine*

Many art house movies do not get mainstream media attention and never become hits. *The Tree Of Life* is an example of an art house movie that did get the public's attention, mostly because of a cast of stars led by Brad Pitt. The movie is about a man looking back at his childhood but also about the origins of all life and our universe. Going back and forth between the two stories, with some sections slow on action, the film was deliberately structured differently than most.

Going All The Way Independent

If you have the money to invest or have someone who wants to finance it, you can try to make the movie yourself. The technology available these days makes it much easier for you to create a film without experience. Wikipedia even offers a wikibook, *The Movie Making Manual*, that outlines filmmaking at **http://en.wikibooks. org/wiki/Movie_Making_Manual**. Still, making your screenplay into a film if you have no experience as a director, cameraperson, or editor is a daunting task. You might know some creative-minded people you can partner with to make the film or to learn the skills you will need to do it yourself. Or you can advertise on the Web for people to collaborate with.

Pitching your movie

Besides querying an agent to get representation for your movie, you can try to work with another type of industry professional. A manager or independent producer also can get your movie made. Managers represent your screenplay but also your whole career as a screenwriter. They will be looking at your screenplay and your package as a whole. How marketable and knowledgeable you are is important to them, as they might be hoping to build a long relationship with you.

You also can look for independent studios to partner with to make your film. An independent studio is a small company, much smaller than a Hollywood studio, which might produce one or two films a year. This type of company might be more likely to review unsolicited manuscripts than a large studio that has plenty of projects. For example, Orlando-based Stars North (**www.stars-north.com**) is an independent movie company that accepts unsolicited manuscripts for short and feature-length films. Or you might have an opportunity to pitch to an independent producer directly. How can you get in touch with these types of small companies? You can search online for them, or use the contacts you have to network.

If you are not having any success with query letters, or you think you can sell yourself and your screenplay well in person, you can look into attending an event designed for aspiring screenwriters to pitch their projects, sometimes called a "pitch fest." These events are usually held in Los Angeles, sometimes as part of a larger conference or event. The Golden Pitch is held in Los Angeles as part of the annual Screenwriting Expo, put together by *Creative Screenwriting* magazine. Screenwriters who buy a ticket get to pitch to a roomful of development executives, producers, and other industry insiders. They will hear your five-minute pitch in small groups and might request that you send your script to them.

If you get an opportunity to pitch your movie to a producer, or even to an agent, practice as much as possible before the event. Keep your pitch as short as possible. The pitch should be just a teaser and stay under two minutes long. If you can get the pitch down to one minute, that is even better. You can tell all the events of your movie in order, as they happen, but that is not likely to be short or attention grabbing. Instead, try to present the major parts of the story in your pitch. Who is the story about? What is important to know about them? What journey will the movie follow them on?

You also can prepare a longer pitch to deliver if asked, which should not exceed ten minutes long. Begin with your logline and then summarize the action of your film, including the incident, plot points, climax, and resolution. Preparing this type of pitch is a new endeavor, and many books and guides exist on how to structure a pitch.

Short Films

Screenwriters increasingly have turned to the Internet to get noticed. Creating a short film and posting it online or submitting it to contests and festivals can help you build a reputation. Many fans routinely create what has become known as "fan fiction" that continues the stories or gives backstory to favorite stories, such as *Star Trek*, *Star Wars*, and *Harry Potter*. Do a quick Google search to see examples of these short films or fan fiction films.

Short film is a somewhat subjective term, with no real rules as to how short or long the film has to be, except that it has to be shorter than a feature film. For Oscar consideration, a short film has to be 40 minutes or less. Short films can be as short as ten minutes long but are more likely to be at least 20 minutes. If you already have written a longer script, you might choose a few scenes from it and create a short film out of a portion of the existing script. You could make the film's ending an ambiguous one that will leave the audience ready for the rest of the film.

A short film can offer you exposure to the same power players you want to gain access to with your feature script. An agent or director can see the short online, or in a contest or festival. It gives you another chance to get your foot in the door besides the endless query letters.

The short film shows your ability to tell a story, albeit in a shorter one, but it still gives anyone who is interested the chance to see a narrative and characters you have created. It also gives you clips and resources to add to your query letters that direct readers to more information about you and what you are capable of doing. Some writers use social media to garner a buzz about their short films. Posting the film to the social media site YouTube® (**www. youtube.com**) exposes it to a worldwide audience that can offer feedback or start a buzz around it. YouTube is a video-sharing website. If you have a YouTube account, you can upload and share movies.

However, if you choose to go this route, be aware of the work this will take. Many people hope to garner attention through social media marketing, and it can take a lot of time to keep updating, posting new comments, sending messages, and finding new friends or getting more people to like your video. You might have to hire someone to do social media marketing for you, as it is a field that grows more complex every day, with new tools and services abounding. Here are some basic steps, however, that you can take on your own:

- Create a Facebook page for yourself as a business that people can like and follow. This allows you to keep those people up to date on what you are doing and where they can see your work and show support for you.

- Join Twitter, or if you already have a twitter account, do some research on how to use it more effectively as a marketing tool.

- Stay on top of emerging social media sites, such as Pinterest®, an online pin board where people share images and videos they like with their friends. Posting to many different sites can allow you to access different audiences.

The equipment you have might be good enough for you to produce a short film. If you have a digital camera, it is most likely capable of taking video. You then can download a free program on your computer to edit the movie clips. Simple, easy to use programs such as iMovie and Windows Movie Maker allow you to cut and re-order clips and add sounds.

Student Films

You can enroll in classes yourself and produce a student film. Going to film school is a serious decision that requires research into which schools in your area and price ranges are the best. Although going to film school will teach you all you need to know about the history and technical aspects of filmmaking, it might not be the right approach for everyone. If you just want to learn aspects of filmmaking, such as camera work or editing, you might be able to take classes through community education, continuing education classes at a local school, or a technical school that specializes in filmmaking. The same goes for basic classes about screenwriting, which are often available through the same organizations. This approach allows you to have instruction and feedback at every stage, and you will learn how to work collaboratively.

However, if you are not a student and are not interested in being one, you can try to collaborate with one. They can provide the knowledge about the technical aspects of filmmaking you may not be familiar with. Also, if they are attending film school, they will be gaining valuable contacts that later can help get your work seen. Post an ad on Craigslist® or on campus message boards to see if you can find someone who sparks your collaborative energy. This partner also might be able to introduce you to more writers with whom you can collaborate. You might be able to form a writing group or even find friends to commiserate about the difficulty of screenwriting with.

Conclusion

here are many reasons to try screenwriting. The idea that has been needling you for years can finally get out on paper, and it might be great. You might develop a new hobby or maybe a passion for writing. If you possess that magical combination of talent, persistence, and luck, you even might find a new, profitable career.

Whether you can succeed at screenwriting depends on more than your ability to write a screenplay. It also depends on how you edit and market the screenplay. It depends on the research you do into the subject matter of the film and into the market for your finished work. It depends on how persistent you can be when it comes time to get an agent to champion your script. But in the end, your success truly depends most of all on the attitude you bring to the job. If you hope to complete a screenplay because you feel passionate about writing or the idea that you have, just getting the script finished is a major accomplishment. Going forward and selling the script is a step you always can take later on.

Being a screenwriter takes many skills: writing, editing, marketing, and determination. But more than anything, after reading this guide, you should have an understanding of what is most important in breaking into screenwriting: persistence. Writing is about craft and skill, but it is also about tenacity. Having the drive to finish your screenplay, even as the editing gets more difficult. Forcing yourself to rewrite, to purge sections that took you a long time to write, can produce feelings akin to those of losing a child. But it is worth it, because in the end, you have a screenplay.

Becoming a screenwriter is a process that does not happen overnight. Setting out to write a screenplay, edit it, polish it, and send it out for sale is a long-term goal. As you begin in this field, you might not know how the new endeavor will turn out. Only by writing the pages can you make the story of you the screenwriter happen.

Good luck to you, and all the best for your screenwriting career.

Resource Guide

his section gives you an idea of where to begin looking online for information on screenwriting. Though all contests and paid services listed here have been verified to be legitimate, they might not be right for your specific script. Conduct some research and make your own decision based on the subject and marketability of your script.

Sample Scripts

Sites where you can find famous movie scripts for reading and reviewing or classic movies to watch:

Simply Scripts
www.simplyscripts.com

Drew's Script-O-Rama
www.script-o-rama.com

The Internet Movie Script Database
www.imsdb.com

Hulu Movies — Mostly known for offering TV shows, Hulu also offers many free movies, including hard-to-find classics
www.hulu.com/movies

About Screenwriting

Sites that talk about the process and craft of screenwriting:

Screenwriters Utopia
www.screenwritersutopia.com

Cinestory — A nonprofit organization that offers fellowships, a contest, and resources for screenwriters
www.cinestory.org

The Writers Store — Online store that offers resources for writers and filmmakers
www.writersstore.com

Hollywood and the Business

Websites and organizations that list the most recent deals and contests for screenwriters in Hollywood:

Done Deal Professional — Reports on the latest deals in Hollywood and around the world. Also has directories of agents and managers
www.donedealpro.com

Scriptapalooza screenplay contest
www.scriptapalooza.com

Movie Bytes — A directory of screenwriting contests
www.moviebytes.com

The Writers Guild of America — Association for working writers. Lots of valuable information on their site that is accessible to non-members
www.wga.org

Trigger Street Labs — Community for screenwriters to critique scripts and offer scripts for critique
http://labs.triggerstreet.com

Talentville — A similar concept to Trigger Street Labs. Screenwriters can upload completed work for review and review work from others.
www.talentville.com

The International Screenwriters Association — Worldwide screenwriting association. Free to join
www.networkisa.org

Working Screenwriters and Industry Insiders

Blogs and official websites of people with an inside view of Hollywood:

SydField.com — Official website of Syd Field, screenwriting guru. Offers information about Syd Field and general information for screenwriters.
www.sydfield.com

Complications Ensue — Blog of TV and film screenwriter Alex Epstein
http://complicationsensue.blogspot.com

Screenwriting from Iowa — Blog of Scott Smith, who details his experiences working as a screenwriter living outside of Hollywood
screenwritingfromiowa.wordpress.com

John August — Official website of screenwriter John August and the Scriptnotes podcast
www.johnaugust.com

The Bitter Script Reader — A blog by a Hollywood script reader that offers advice on scripts
http://thebitterscriptreader.blogspot.com

Go Into The Story — Blog of Scott Meyers, screenwriting teacher and former Hollywood writer and producer
www.gointothestory.com

The Aspiring TV Writer and Screenwriter — Blog by a working script reader about her real life experiences trying to break into screenwriting
http://aspiringtvwriter.blogspot.com

Scriptwriting in the UK — Blog by Danny Stack, a working writer and director
http://dannystack.blogspot.com

Downloads

Free downloads that can be useful for screenwriters:

Abode Premiere Pro — Movie making software. Download a free 30-day trial.
www.adobe.com/cfusion/tdrc/index.cfm?product= premiere_pro

Final Cut Pro — Movie editing software for Apple OS. Free 30-day trial
www.apple.com/finalcutpro/trial

Scrivener — Writing software for Apple OS. Free trial available.
www.literatureandlatte.com/scrivener.php

Join.me — A useful software for collaboration. Allows you to remotely see someone else's computer screen
https://join.me

Author Biography

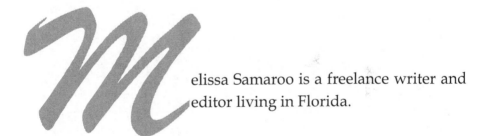

elissa Samaroo is a freelance writer and editor living in Florida.

Index